ZELDA
AN ILLUSTRATED LIFE

Success was the goal for this generation and to a startling extent they

have attained it, and now we venture to say that, if intimately approached,

nine in ten would confess that success is only a decoration they wished to

wear: what they really wanted is something deeper and richer than that.

—Zelda Sayre Fitzgerald "Looking Back Eight Years," *College Humor* · 1928

ZELDA
AN ILLUSTRATED LIFE

THE PRIVATE WORLD
OF ZELDA FITZGERALD

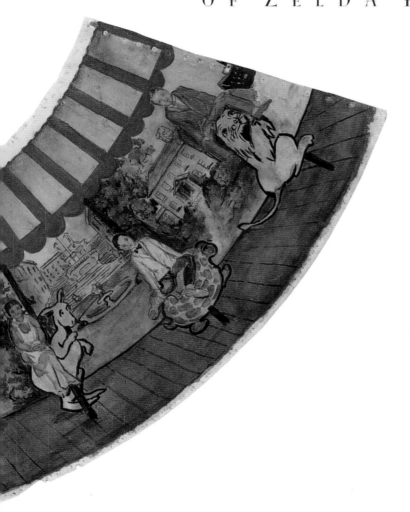

Edited by Eleanor Lanahan
Essays by Peter Kurth and Jane S. Livingston

Harry N. Abrams, Inc., Publishers

Developed and produced by
Verve Editions, Burlington, Vermont

Gary Chassman · Julie Stillman

Designed by Robert A. Yerks

Library of Congress Cataloging–in–Publication Data

Fitzgerald, Zelda, 1900–1948.
  Zelda, an illustrated life : the private world of Zelda Fitzgerald
/ edited by Eleanor Lanahan : essays by Peter Kurth and Jane
Livingston.
      p.   cm.
  ISBN 0–8109–3983–5 (clothbound)
    1. Fitzgerald, Zelda, 1900–1948. 2. Women and literature—United
States—History—20th century. 3. Women authors. American—20th
century—Biography. 4. Women artists—United States—Biography.
5. Dancers—United States—Biography. I. Lanahan, Eleanor Anne, [date].
II. Title.
PS3511.I9234Z33 1996
813'.52—dc20
[B]   95–38940

Selected excerpts are reprinted with permission of Scribner,
a Division of Simon & Schuster, from *Zelda Fitzgerald:
The Collected Writings*, ed. by Matthew J. Bruccoli. Copyright
© 1991 by the Trustees under Agreement dated July 3, 1975,
Created by Frances Scott Fitzgerald Smith.

Photograph Credits

page 1: Sketch (portrait of Zelda) by James Montgomery Flagg for
  CollegeHumor magazine, 1928. Courtesy National Portrait
  Gallery. The Smithsonian Institution.

page 5: Zelda's ostrich feather fan. Courtesy of the L.B.J. Library,
  University of Texas.

pages 10, 14, 17, 18, 20, 23, 24: Courtesy of Visual Materials Division,
  Dept. of Rare Books and Special Collections, Princeton
  University Libraries.

pages 13, 78: From Arthur Mizener, *Scott Fitzgerald and His World*,
  (New York, 1972), pp. 86, 88.

pages 28, 29: From *The Romantic Egoists*, ed. by Matthew J. Bruccoli, Scottie
  Fitzgerald Smith, and Joan P. Kerr. (New York, 1974), p. 169.

page 79: Charles Demuth, *Bird Woman*. Courtesy of Kennedy Gallery,
  New York.

page 81: John Marin, *Mid-Manhattan #1*. Courtesy of Nathan Emory
  Coffin Collection of the Des Moines Art Center 1961.29.
  John Marin, *Region of the Brooklyn Bridge Fantasy*.
  Courtesy of the Whitney Museum, New York.

pages 82-83: From M. Boutet de Monvel, *Joan of Arc*, (New York, 1923).

page 84: From Paul Louis de Giafferri, *L'Histoire du Costume Feminin
  Francais de l'an 1037 a l'an 1870*, (Paris, 1929).

page 85: From J. Pinchon, *L'Enfance de Becassine*, (Paris, 1926).

Overleaf · Lampshade

c. 1928 · 19 x 42 in.
Courtesy of Samuel J. Lanahan

Painted by Zelda at Ellerslie in Delaware, the lampshade depicts many places where the family had lived — Villa St Louis, Juan-les-Pins, France; White Bear Lake Yacht Club, Minnesota; Ellerslie, Delaware; the Plaza Hotel; Capri; the Villa Marie at St Raphaël, the Spanish Steps; the house in Westport, Connecticut.

Riding the merry-go-round are the family, servants, and friends, including "Nanny" on the mouse, Zelda on the rooster, Scottie on the horse, Scott on the elephant, Tana the butler on the turtle, and (most likely) George Jean Nathan on the lion.

Acknowledgments

Many people have contributed to the realization of this book. My sister and brother, Cecilia Ross and Samuel Lanahan, lent encouragement and shared the expense. I owe a debt to all the people who contributed time, historical clues and assistance: Margaret Ausfeld, Duncan Black, Louise Brooks, Alice Carter, Janie Cohen, Margaret and William Cradduck, Anne Graffeo, John Hartsfield, Mickey Ingalls, Mary Adair Dockery, Arlyn Bruccoli, Kristina Fares, Neil Fulghum, Diane and Joe Kalman, Marie Kalman, Christina Kelly, Deede Lovette, Leslie and Julian McPhillips, Helen Means, Ted Mitchell, Dr Natchez Morice Jr, Kathy Nagler, Kitty and Charles Nicrosi, Mary Bear Norman, Richard Ober, Ann Porter, Carolyn Shafer, Don Skemer, Louise Stephaich, Dana Sutton, Marsha Weber, and Janice Wright.

Zelda's Fan

This ostrich feather fan was an engagement present from Scott in 1919. He purchased it with the proceeds from the sale of his first short story to the *Saturday Evening Post*.

ents

Preface

T HIS IS THE FIRST BOOK DEDICATED EXCLUSIVELY TO ZELDA FITZGERALD'S ART. ALTHOUGH SOME OF HER PAINTINGS HAVE BEEN EXHIBITED OVER THE YEARS, ONLY RECENTLY HAVE HER ACCOMPLISHMENTS BEEN AFFORDED THE RESPECT THEY DESERVE.

The first large exhibition of Zelda's paintings was held in 1974, twenty-six years after her death. The Montgomery Museum of Fine Arts hosted the event soon after my mother, Scottie Fitzgerald Smith, moved to Alabama, bringing with her more than 100 of her mother's paper dolls and paintings. The Museum contributed four paintings that Zelda had given them. Johns Hopkins University sent seven gouaches. Another seventeen works were loaned by individuals. The show was well received. A small catalogue was produced, including some dozen black-and-white illustrations, but it proved too small a printing to supply all the visitors. The exhibition traveled to Mobile before most of the paintings lapsed back into the obscurity of private collections.

Ballerinas Dressing
c. 1941

A sampling of Zelda's paintings was reproduced in *The Romantic Egoists*, a pictorial "autobiography" of Scott and Zelda, which my mother coauthored with Joan Kerr and Prof. Matthew Bruccoli in 1974.

In June of 1980 the National Portrait Gallery in Washington paid tribute to the Jazz Age with an exhibition entitled, "Zelda and Scott: The Beautiful and Damned." The show focused on portraits of the Fitzgeralds and their friends from the gallery's collection, as well as Zelda's design for the cover of *The Beautiful and Damned*, paper dolls of the family, and her biographical lampshade. Since then, little of Zelda's art has been available to a wide audience.

When my mother died in 1986, her collection was divided between we three children and the Montgomery Museum of Fine Arts. Zelda's art, often given only token consideration by biographers, was in peril of being scattered and forgotten.

It wasn't until Carolyn Shafer, in the course of writing her dissertation at the University of South Carolina on the art of Zelda Fitzgerald, called me

Zelda Sayre · 1918

with a few questions and alerted me to the whereabouts of many undocumented works, that the idea of a book was sparked. She provided me with clues to the location of many of the original paintings. A few pieces had changed hands; some, unfortunately, had vanished. There were also some wonderful discoveries. I had my first glimpse of eleven of Zelda's art therapy exercises, donated to Harvard's Busch-Reisinger Museum by the widow of Dr Fredric Wertham, a special consultant at the Phipps Psychiatric Clinic in Baltimore. Exciting, too, was tracking down some of the far-flung pages of Zelda's sketchbooks that an art dealer had rescued after her death. A sequence of phone calls netted a painting that had been part of Zelda's exhibition at the Cary Ross Gallery in 1934 — stored in an attic in Palm Beach.

When I first presented the idea for a book to Gary Chassman and Julie Stillman of Verve Editions, they were surprised and delighted by the quality of Zelda's art. They agreed to develop and produce *Zelda · An Illustrated Life* and to mastermind its organization; their enthusiasm and hard work are largely responsible for its existence. These pages were enlivened by the fine aesthetic sense of the designer, Robert Yerks.

Once we had selected the paintings, we needed to recruit appropriate writers to illuminate Zelda's life and art. To that end, we asked two especially qualified people to contribute essays. Peter Kurth, author of three biographies: *American Cassandra: The Life of Dorothy Thompson, Anastasia: The Riddle of Anna Anderson*, and *Tsar: The Lost World of Nicholas and Alexandra*, has produced a masterful and spirited portrait of Zelda. Jane Livingston's experience as chief curator of the Corcoran Gallery of Art and her extensive knowledge of art history, enabled her to provide insights into Zelda's paintings and to place her work into its proper historical context.

At last, this book, and the exhibition it accompanies, comprise a reunion of Zelda's best. It is my hope that it will present, for the first time, a unified view of Zelda's art and provide a valuable dimension to understanding her multifaceted spirit.

E. L.

Introduction

Eleanor Lanahan

*Both of us are very splashy vivid pictures, those kind with the details left out,
but I know our colors will blend, and I think we'll look very well hanging beside
each other in the gallery of life.*

—Zelda wrote Scott in February 1920, two months before their wedding

Zelda Sayre arrived with the century, on July 24, 1900. The youngest of six children, her desires were indulged by a doting mother. Zelda seemed licensed at birth to express the freedom and romance of the fictional gypsy for whom she was named. Born into a society that cultivated femininity to an art form if not a strict code of conduct, Zelda, a prankster and tomboy, was redeemed by her gift for whiplash observation, grace, and a kindness that ran deep as her marrow.

As a teenager, she showed talent as a writer, ballet dancer, and mischievous flirt. By eighteen she was the belle of Montgomery, Alabama. At the age of twenty, she married the promising young Yankee author, F. Scott Fitzgerald, and moved to New York City. That same year, Scott's first novel, *This Side of Paradise*, was published, and Zelda shared the celebrity of his early success.

In 1921 the Fitzgeralds only child was born, a daughter named Scottie. Throughout the ensuing decade, the family moved from New York, to France, to Delaware, and back to France — on a spree that earned them as much notoriety for the way they lived as for what they accomplished. During the exuberant early years of their marriage, Zelda kept a lively diary, dabbled in painting, contributed social commentary to *Metropolitan Magazine*, *McCall's* and the *New York Tribune*, and manifested not one whit of interest in the domestic arts. Scott, greatly inspired by his singular wife, wrote of their expatriate adventures, "One could get away with more on the summer Riviera, and whatever happened seemed to have something to do with art." Between France and Italy, he finished his masterpiece, *The Great Gatsby*. But Zelda was no longer content to be the decorative appendage of her famous husband; she began to crave an outlet for her talents and recognition of her own. On Capri, in early 1925, she is reported to have taken her first painting lessons — the one art she pursued to the end of her days.

Zelda died in March of 1948, just two months after I was born. Revealing that Zelda was my grandmother dates her horribly; she hardly lived long enough to be one. Although we never met, it has always been as if her fresh, youthful scent lingered in our house. Throughout my childhood her cityscapes animated the walls of our sunporch and living room, surrounding us with a curious nostalgia for the boulevards of Manhattan and Paris, full of commotion and color — and with illustrious landmarks painted from memory.

A few of Zelda's paintings from fairy tales and *Alice's Adventures in Wonderland* inhabited our bedrooms, but most of her artwork spent almost five decades in one attic or another — preserved in tattered cardboard portfolios. In the fifties and sixties we grandchildren granted ourselves permission to rifle through these fragile artifacts. Zelda's compositions were so suggestive of dramatic stage sets — her use of primary colors so bold — that I sensed, even then, the reckless poetry of her every endeavor.

Few people know that Zelda painted casually during the nomadic years of her marriage, and seriously

Zelda and Scott Fitzgerald · c. 1921

throughout the last fourteen years of her life. But for anyone who is acquainted with Zelda's writing, it should come as no surprise that she painted. Her prose, like her art, is lush, vibrant and original. There is a pirouette to her language; her descriptions are often saturated with sensual, visual metaphor. Scott was so impressed by the freshness of her observations that he occasionally looted her letters and diaries in search of uncommon expression. An excerpt from her novel *Save Me the Waltz* illustrates Zelda's tactile vernacular:

> Yellow roses she bought with her money like Empire satin brocade, and white lilacs and pink tulips like molded confectioner's frosting, and deep-red roses like a Villon poem, black and velvety as an insect wing, the crystalline drops of lily of the valley, a bowl of nasturtiums like beaten brass, anemones pieced out of wash material, and malignant parrot tulips scratching the air with their jagged barbs, and the voluptuous scrambled convolutions of Parma violets. She bought lemon-yellow carnations perfumed with the taste of hard candy, and garden roses purple as raspberry puddings, and every kind of white flower the florist knew how to grow. She gave Madame gardenias like white kid gloves and forget-me-nots from the Madeleine stalls, threatening sprays of gladioli, and the soft, even purr of black tulips. She bought flowers like salads and flowers like fruits, jonquils and narcissus, poppies and ragged robins, and flowers with the brilliant carnivorous qualities of Van Gogh …

With another splash of the pen, in "The Millionaire's Girl," a story written just before her breakdown in 1930, Zelda describes New York City:

> Twilights were wonderful just after the war. They hung above New York like indigo wash, forming themselves from asphalt dust and sooty shadows under the cornices and limp gusts of air exhaled from closing windows, to hang above the streets with all the mystery of white fog rising off a swamp. The faraway lights from buildings high in the sky burned hazily through the blue, like golden objects lost in deep grass, and the noise of hurrying streets took on that hushed quality of many footfalls in a huge stone square …

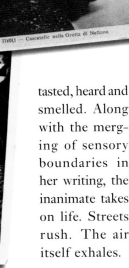

Her literary descriptions display a synthesis of the senses — as if one sensation were readily translatable to another — as if, for Zelda, colors were being simultaneously tasted, heard and smelled. Along with the merging of sensory boundaries in her writing, the inanimate takes on life. Streets rush. The air itself exhales.

Romance, too, permeates her letters and painting. After the Civil War, when the South experienced an acute shortage of men and money, acquiring a husband became a matter of survival for a young woman, and much artfulness was deployed toward that aim. Zelda's romantic impulses, partly instilled by a culture that emphasized the importance of being beguiling, mysterious, and somewhat helpless, often served to sweeten a bitter reality.

At the age of twenty-seven she undertook the study of ballet — far too late an age to become the superior dancer she so desperately wanted to be. For three grueling years she practiced — often eight hours a day — sacrificing almost all home life to her passion.

Zelda's first breakdown closely coincided with the sudden stock market crash in America. After April 1930, when she was first admitted to a clinic, Zelda and Scott were besieged by emotional, marital and financial difficulties. In "A Couple of Nuts," a story published in 1932, she fictionalized the onset of the family's many misfortunes:

> In those days of going to pieces and general disintegration it was charming to see them together. Their friends were divided into two camps as to whose stamina it was that kept them going and comparatively equilibrated in that crazy world of ours playing at prisoner's base across the Atlantic Ocean.

In a letter to Scott soon after she was hospitalized at the Prangins Clinic in Switzerland, she explained her breakdown in sensory terms:

Every day it seems to me that things are more barren and hopeless — in Paris, before I realized that I was sick, there was a new significance to everything: stations and streets and facades of buildings — colors were infinite, part of the air, and not restricted by the lines that encompassed them and lines were free of the masses they held. There was music that beat behind my forehead and other music that fell into my stomach from a high parabola and there was some Schumann that was still and tender…. Then the world became embryonic in Africa — and there was no need for communication. The Arabs fermenting in the vastness; the curious quality of their eyes and the smell of ants; a detachment as if I was on the other side of black gauze—

Scott felt that Zelda's obsession with dance had been her undoing — Zelda agreed to cease dancing but implored him to forswear drink. Both expressed bitter disappointment in their marriage, but their reproaches were always mingled with the stronger currents of love and concern. Again from Prangins, she wrote Scott:

If all the kisses and love I'm sending you arrive at their destination you will be as worn away as St Peter's toe and by the time I arrive have practically no features left at all — but I shall know you always by the lilt in your darling person.

Despite an agonizing eighteen months in Switzerland, during which she was diagnosed as schizophrenic, Zelda's letters to Scott often evoked romantic settings:

The moon slips into the mountains like a lost penny and the fields are black and pungent and I want you near so that I [can] touch you in the autumn stillness even a little bit like the last echo of summer…. Anyway, I love you the most and you 'phoned me just because you 'phoned me to-night — I walked on those telephone wires for two hours after holding your love like a parasol to balance me. My dear—

Zelda and Scottie · c. 1933

Even in her darkest moments, Zelda made crystalline observations:

When I came down the hill the moon was still and heavy spreading out the meadows and the warmth of day hid musty under the trees but over the wheat field the air was as walking in a mist — I love those deep dead moons that creep under things and gouge great shadows over the lawns and clip the tops of foliage. I wished we were walking to-gether, quietly.

Scott and Zelda's lives and writing are inextricably entwined. He encouraged her to write, offered editorial insights, and helped place her work with publishers. But to almost the same degree he encouraged her self-expression, he inhibited it.

Zelda began working on *Save Me the Waltz* in 1931 when her doctors pronounced her, if not cured, in a state of remission. The family returned from Europe to settle in Montgomery. Within a month Scott departed for Hollywood to work on a script for Metro-Goldwyn-Mayer. During the eight weeks he was gone, Zelda launched a novel and finished seven stories — one of which was published by *Scribner's Magazine*. For inspiration, she also read one of Scott's stories every night.

The first draft of *Save Me the Waltz* was completed by March 1932, after a mere five months of labor. Midway through the project, however, Zelda suffered a second breakdown and was hospitalized at the Phipps Psychiatric Clinic, a part of Johns Hopkins Hospital in Baltimore. She continued to struggle to establish her own identity as a writer, but reminded Scott of her utter dependence on him:

I have often told you that I am that little fish who swims about under a shark and, I believe, lives indelicately on its offal. Anyway, that is the way I am.... I adore you and worship you and I am miserable that you be made even temporarily unhappy by those divergencies of direction in myself which I cannot satisfactorily explain and which leave me eternally alone except for you and baffled.

The first version of her novel was a source of friction between the Fitzgeralds, utilizing as it did, some of the same material about mental illness that Scott was using in his novel-in-progress, *Tender Is the Night*. Reluctantly, before publication, Zelda agreed to subordinate her claim to her autobiographical material to her husband's. The final version of *Save Me the Waltz*,

published by Scribners in October 1932, makes no mention of the heroine's psychological instability, otherwise it comprises an almost transparent self-portrait. In four sections Zelda recounts the story of Alabama Knight, her youth, her marriage to an accomplished painter, her aspiration to dance ballet in Paris, and her eventual return to the more familiar and balanced atmosphere of the South.

When the novel was finished, Zelda embarked on another, but abandoned it when Scott again objected to the severe overlapping of their material. Instead, she wrote and produced a play in Baltimore called *Scandalabra*. Even with Scott's editorial assistance, the play was a rambling, three-hour disaster.

The daily two hours of painting that her doctors had recommended for therapy became an important refuge from other disappointments. In October 1933, Zelda participated in the Independents' Show in Baltimore and began a period of intense artistic productivity.

Zelda and Scottie · 1922

Zelda's third breakdown in early 1934 led to her hospitalization at Craig House clinic in Beacon, New York. To raise her spirits, Scott organized an exhibition of her paintings at the Cary Ross Gallery in Manhattan, which was scheduled to coordinate with the publication of *Tender Is the Night*. One month before the show, Zelda, who was painting fervently, and producing a series of painfully distorted figures, wrote Scott:

Please ask Mrs. Owens [Scott's secretary] to hurry with my paints. There are so many winter trees exhibiting irresistible intricacies, and there are many neo-classic columns, and there are gracious expanses of snow and the brooding quality of a gray and heavy sky, all of which makes me want terribly to paint....

This is a beautiful place; there is everything on earth available and I have a little room to paint in with a window higher than my head the way I like windows to be. When they are that way, you can look out on the sky and feel like Faust in his den, or an ancient alchemist or anybody you like.

Scott, concerned that Zelda's former obsession with dance was being transposed only to a ruinous intensity about art, received this reassurance:

Zelda and her grandson, Thomas · June 1947

Dear: I am not trying to make myself into a great artist or a great anything. Though you persist in thinking that an exaggerated ambition is the fundamental cause of my collapse, knowing the motivating elements that now make me wa[nt] to work I cannot agree with you and Dr Forel — though of course, the will-to-power may have played a part in the very beginning. However, five years have passed since then, and one matures. I do the things I can do and that interest me and if you'd like me to give up everything I like to do I will do so willingly if it will advance matters any. I am not headstrong and do not like existing entirely at other peoples expense and being a constant care to others any better than you like my being in such a situation.

If you feel that it is an imposition on Cary to have the exhibition, the pictures can wait. I believe in them and in Emerson's theory about good-workman-ship. If they are good, they will come to light some day.

Before the exhibition, Zelda also wrote a reminiscence piece, "Show Mr. and Mrs. F. to Number___," in which she sweeps poetically through practically every hotel that she and Scott had ever patronized. At the end, she refers to a recent visit to New York:

We saw Georgia O'Keeffe's pictures and it was a deep emotional experience to abandon oneself to that majestic aspiration so adequately fitted into eloquent abstract forms.

The article, which appeared in *Esquire* in May 1934, was one of her last two published works. From that time forth, Zelda focused her creativity primarily on painting. The New York exhibition received disappointing reviews. Her friend Sara Murphy bought *Chinese Theater* and Dorothy Parker bought a portrait of Scott called *The Coronet Player*. Maxwell Perkins, Scott's editor, bought *The Plaid Shirt* — all of these paintings have since vanished. Only one work from the show, *Au Claire de la Lune*, purchased by Tommy Hitchcock, can be located; apparently Zelda's patrons pitied her and disposed of their purchases.

In the following decade she participated in a handful of group exhibitions and gave most of her paintings away — to my mother, to friends, and to her doctors. Years later, by way of explaining what she considered her lack of accomplishment, she wrote my mother [Scottie]:

I had few friends but I never quarreled with any; save once with a friend in the Paris Opera whom I loved. Daddy loved glamour & so I also had a great respect for popular acclaim. I wish that I had been able to do better one thing & not so give[n] to running into cul-de-sac with so many.

Not only had Zelda been torn between mediums, but in *Save Me the Waltz*, Alabama explains another division, this one psychological:

Yes — but David, it's very difficult to be
two simple people at once, one who

15

wants to have a law to itself and the other who wants to keep all the nice old things and be loved and safe and protected.

After a period of withdrawal and terrible hallucinations, Zelda received what she believed was a direct communication from God. Along with it came an imperative to preach His doctrine. In this phase of her illness, she was believed to have a religious mania, and Scott relinquished hope of her eventual recovery. She was transferred back to the Sheppard-Pratt Hospital in May 1934. Five months later, she wrote him:

The Sheppard-Pratt Hospital is located somewhere in the hinterlands of the human consciousness and I can be located there any time between the dawn of consciousness and the beginning of old age.

Darling: Life is difficult. There are so many problems. 1) The problem of how to stay here and 2) The problem of how to get out.

She ended the letter with a sketch of Scott in Guatemala, and a request for him to take her there (opposite).

In April 1936, Scott arranged for Zelda to move to the slightly more affordable Highland Hospital in Asheville, North Carolina. He was then living in nearby Tryon, taking a cure for what he believed to be tuberculosis. But the Fitzgeralds lived in proximity to each other for a relatively short while. In late 1937, Scott received a badly needed offer to work as a salaried screenwriter in Hollywood and moved to California. Scottie stayed East — at boarding school and then, in 1939, at Vassar College. Zelda was now permanently separated from both her husband and daughter. Her last glimpse of Scott was in early 1939 when he met her in Asheville and took her on a brief trip to Cuba. Over the course of the holiday he got so drunk that Zelda had to arrange for him to be hospitalized. She returned to Highlands alone, making no mention of her chaperon's behavior to hospital authorities, and for this discretion Scott later thanked her:

Self-portrait
Early 1940s · Pencil on paper · 11 × 9 in.
Courtesy of the Scott & Zelda Fitzgerald Museum, Montgomery, Alabama

...you are the finest, loveliest, tenderest, most beautiful person I have ever known, but even that is an understatement because the length that you went to there at the end would have tried anybody beyond endurance.

In 1940, Zelda's doctors finally agreed that she was capable of living outside of the hospital. She returned to Montgomery, as an outpatient, and wrote Scott:

I don't write; and I don't paint: largely because it requires most of my resources to keep out of the hospital. I've had such a difficult struggle over the last ten years that making the social adjustment is more difficult than I had supposed.

we /sup to thank you for your trouble
about the books — you are so good to us.

Love, Sweetheart

Zelda

P.S. Dolli
cook and so
forth, and maybe
discover gold
if you will
take me to
Guatemala - or
are you too busy.
Do-Do in Guatemala
Love.

Scott Fitzgerald
From a letter to him dated October 1934

It was a source of sadness that she could not be more of a mother, but Zelda was delighted when Scottie married, and sent her housekeeping advice—indicative of her abiding insouciance for the domestic arts:

There isn't any real reason sheets should be white: pink sheets would be most entertaining and one could sew the strips together with narrow embroidery... Don't buy all the spoons and sauce-pans which one always seems to need... They breed under the kitchen sink if left to themselves

With the birth of her grandson, Thomas Lanahan, in 1946, Zelda had finally found her niche. She went to work making him a portfolio of paper dolls and instructive Bible illustrations.

By then, my mother was living in New York City. She encouraged Zelda, whose financial situation was austere, to paint landscapes — subjects she knew she could readily sell through a gallery in Manhattan. But Zelda pursued her own fancy, producing religious works and other items that my mother felt had little commercial appeal.

Most of Zelda's surviving paintings were done in the forties. They give testimony to her full life: the fairy-tale-like quality of her youth, the glamour and romance of her years in New York and Paris, the turbulence of her inner life, her deep religious commitment, her meditative appreciation of landscape and flowers, and, in the Alice in Wonderland series, her high-spirited sense of absurdity. It's a shame she isn't around to see her paintings come to light, almost a century after her birth, but I suspect she would be deeply gratified.

For months at a time, Zelda was now able to live quietly at her mother's house, and eventually established a studio in the garage. She and Scott corresponded regularly. She wrote him nostalgic letters about the past, and of her hopes for a meeting. They shared their concerns about Scottie, about art, and about the perennial issue of money. In December 1940, Scott died suddenly of a heart attack at the age of forty-four.

Zelda remained tormented by cycles of illness until the end of her life. During her last eight years, she lived quietly as the God-fearing, unpredictable, and valiantly cheerful widow of a temporarily forgotten author.

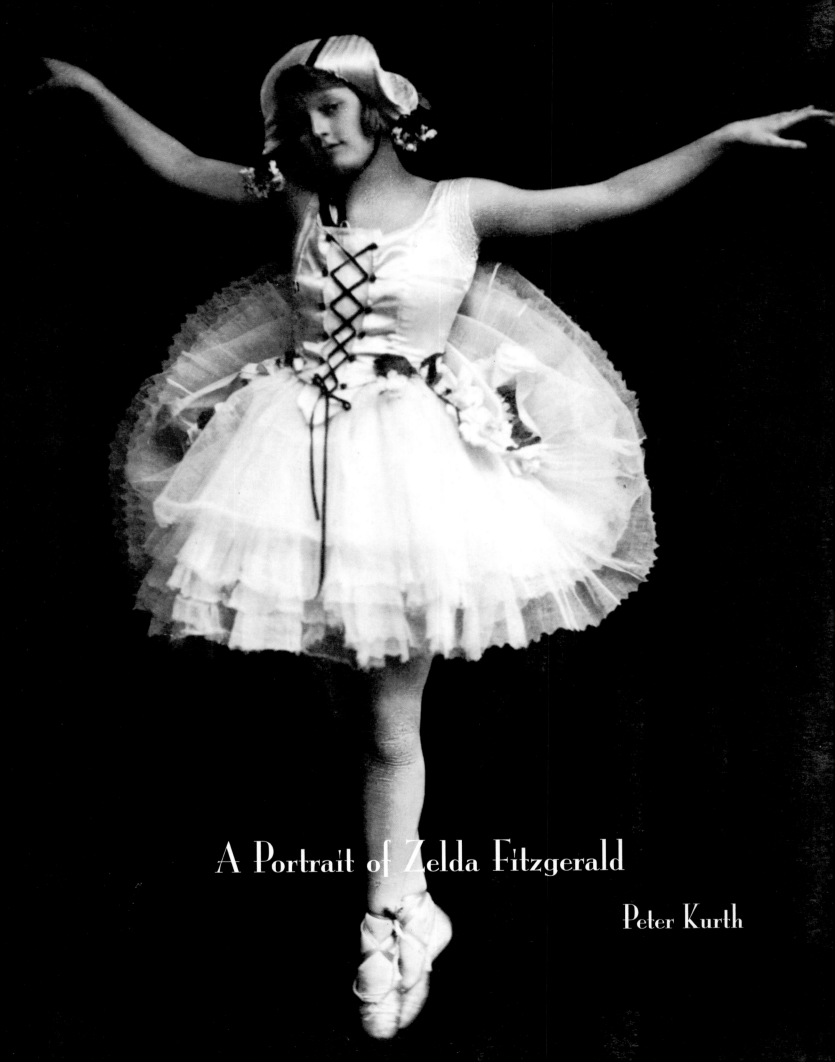

A Portrait of Zelda Fitzgerald

Peter Kurth

I don't need anything except hope, which I can't find
by looking backwards or forwards,
so I suppose the thing is to shut my eyes.

—Zelda Sayre Fitzgerald

In the spring of 1919, about a year before they were married, Zelda Sayre wrote her fiancé, F. Scott Fitzgerald, from Montgomery, Alabama:

I've spent to-day in the grave-yard — It really isn't a cemetery, you know — trying to unlock a rusty iron vault built in the side of the hill. It's all washed and covered with weepy, watery blue flowers that might have grown from dead eyes — sticky to touch with a sickening odor — The boys wanted to get in to test my nerve — to-night — I wanted to feel *"William Wreford, 1864." Why should graves make people feel in vain? I've heard that so much, and Grey is so convincing, but somehow I can't find anything hopeless in having lived — All the broken columns and clasped hands and doves and angels mean romances and in a hundred years I think I shall like having young people speculate on whether my eyes were brown or blue — of course, they are neither — I hope my grave has an air of many, many years ago about it — Isn't it funny how, out of a row of Confederate soldiers, two or three will make you think of dead lovers and dead loves — when they're exactly like the others, even to the yellowish moss? Old death is so beautiful — so very beautiful — We will die together — I know —*

Sweetheart—

They did not die together: Scott Fitzgerald succumbed to a heart attack in Hollywood in 1940, at the age of forty-four, while Zelda, having survived him by eight years, perished in a midnight fire at a mental hospital in North Carolina, where she was undergoing treatment for schizophrenia. Since 1932, the Fitzgeralds had effectively been separated, after Zelda's second major breakdown and Scott's calamitous degeneration into alcoholism and literary oblivion.

"It was despair, despair, despair," Scott wrote. "In a real dark night of the soul it is always three o'clock in the morning, day after day." When he died, as his daughter, Scottie, remembered, "he couldn't have found a book of his in any bookstore; he probably couldn't even have asked for one without getting a blank stare from the saleslady." Zelda, described in the newspapers as Scott's "invalid wife," was "not able to attend" his funeral in Rockville, Maryland. For a number of years, to the extent that her illness allowed it, she had been living again in Montgomery, and sitting again, "when she felt quite alone," among the moldering Confederate graves. But now she was a Christian — a born-again apostle of the Lord — bubbling over with words and warnings about the onerous path to salvation.

"The world angered God with vanities and its indulgences," Zelda proclaimed, "and the world existed in time-steeped, blood-saturated, glory-worn abeyance of His Grace." No one in her hometown knew exactly what to make of Zelda's religious mania. She had a complicated reputation, to say the least: first (and foremost, this being the South) as "a Sayre," the daughter of one of Alabama's finest families and a kind of local royalty; then as the glamorous, madcap, much-publicized wife of one of America's most famous authors; and now, in her disturbance, as "that crazy woman" — a phrase Zelda was likely to hear only from a distance, whispered by strangers or yelled out by children as she

Zelda at age 15

walked or bicycled through town. A middle-aged woman in heavy stockings and an Alpine hat riding a bike in the heat of summer was a strange enough sight in Montgomery; Zelda bicycled all year round, and when she wasn't cycling she was walking — striding — for stretches of five or ten miles at a time.

"There goes that crazy woman," people remarked. "Momma says she's not right in the head." One afternoon, unexpectedly, Zelda was discovered in the library of a friend's house in Montgomery, quietly reading and drinking wine. She apologized for the intrusion, but said it was the only place in town where she could sit by herself "and take a drink and read." A young man who knew her at the end of her life got the feeling that she "didn't see many people anymore.... She would talk about the past: her reveries were always in the past and her mind often turned to Paris, which she loved. Then she would talk about Scott and Hemingway. But she spoke very little about herself."

"Of course at first she was invited to parties," said one of Zelda's friends after her return to Alabama. "I remember one she came to. Everyone was standing in the garden with drinks in their hands and when Zelda saw them she dropped to her knees in prayer. You can imagine how that ripped Montgomery." In a letter to Anne Ober, the wife of Scott Fitzgerald's literary agent, Zelda admitted that she sometimes felt "desperately sad" when she thought about former times, about Paris and Scott and the golden triumphs of the 1920s. But then, she explained, "I reconciled myself and had to accept with grace the implacable exigencies of life. I would not exchange my experience for any other because it has brought me the

Dust jacket photograph for *Save Me the Waltz*

knowledge of God." It would be nice, she added, in one of those stunning non sequiturs that always distinguished her speech, if someone would send her a valentine. Zelda had *always* "ripped Montgomery."

As a young girl, while still in her teens, she was the belle of every county, every ball, and every town in Alabama — "a kingmaker," her admirers said, "an American value," "the prettiest girl in Alabama *and* Georgia." "When Zelda Sayre came to dances, the Birmingham girls just went on home," one of her rivals recalled. "No more hope for a dance that evening." Edmund Wilson later described Zelda as "a Barbarian princess from the South," while she herself was content to be called "a Southern girl [moving] brightly along high places."

"She has the straightest nose, the most determined little chin, and the bluest eyes in Montgomery," said an Alabama newspaper. "She might dance like Pavlova if her nimble feet were not so busy keeping up with the pace of a string of young but ardent admirers." In the general opinion of Montgomery society Zelda Sayre was also wild and "reckless," but, after all, she was Judge A. D. Sayre's youngest child, Mrs Sayre's "Baby" and her favorite, and it would have been hard to keep her in line under any circumstances. She described herself when young as "independent," "courageous," and "without a thought for anyone else.... I did not have a single feeling of inferiority, or shyness, or doubt, and no moral principles." By the time she turned eighteen she was already drinking (and drinking heavily), smoking cigarettes and bobbing her hair. "She lived on the cream at the top of the bottle," in the words of one of her swains, even before she met

Fitzgerald in 1918, when the First World War brought hordes and swarms of servicemen to Camp Sheridan in Alabama.

They met at a country club dance in Montgomery in July of that year, when Scott was a 1st Lieutenant in the 67th Infantry and Zelda, having just graduated from high school, was already "engaged" unofficially to a wide assortment of men. "The Ohio troops have started a wild and heated correspondence with Montgomery damsels," she wrote Scott on one of his extended trips north. "From all I can gather, the whole 37th Div will be down in May — Then I guess the butterflies will flitter a trifle more." The records of the Fitzgeralds' courtship — carried on mainly by letter when the war was over — are filled with Zelda's assurances that she loved "only" him ("and I want to be married soon ... Don't say I'm not enthusiastic — You ought to know"), and Scott's ever more desperate references to princesses in towers: he wanted Zelda kept in one, in other words. She had slept with him almost immediately after their first meeting, leaving Scott only to wonder "how many more" there had been. He was a great self-doubter, and a hypochondriac, and nothing Zelda ever said could put his mind at ease.

"I've always known that any girl who gets stewed in public, who frankly enjoys and tells shocking stories, who smokes constantly and makes the remark that she has 'kissed thousands of men and intends to kiss thousands more,' cannot be considered beyond reproach even if above it," Scott wrote. "...I fell in love with her courage, her sincerity and her flaming self-respect and it's these things I'd believe in even if the whole world indulged in wild suspicions that she wasn't all that she should be.... I love her and that's the beginning and end of everything." Meantime Zelda made no effort to hide her various romantic attachments.

"Eleanor Browder and I have found a syndicate," she told Scott, "and we're 'best friends' to more college boys than Solomon had wives.... I have always been inclined toward masculinity. It's such a cheery atmosphere boys radiate — And we do such unique things." A "wholesome amour" with a "startling quarterback" did not go unmentioned, and when Scott protested too strongly about Zelda's apparent promiscuity she nearly lost her temper on the page:

Scott, you're really awful silly — In the first place, I haven't kissed anybody good-bye, and in the second place, nobody's left in the first place — You know, darling, that I love you too much to want to. If I did have an honest — or dishonest — desire to kiss just one or two people, I might — but I couldn't ever want to — my mouth is yours. But s'pose I did — Don't you know it'd just be absolutely nothing — Why can't you understand that nothing means anything except your darling self and your love — I wish we'd hurry and I'd be yours so you'd know.

In his hometown of St Paul, Minnesota, Scott was putting the finishing touches on what became *This Side of Paradise*, his first published book and a runaway success. "Zelda was cagey about throwing in her lot with me before I was a money-maker," said Scott, and indeed, while she liked to insist that "material things are nothing," Zelda remained cold to the thought of "a sordid, colorless existence" as the wife of a starving author. She broke the engagement formally at least once, but finally consented to the wedding in April 1920, when *This Side of Paradise* took New York by storm. Many years later, in a letter to a friend, Zelda listed the main criteria at the back of her decision to marry Scott:

1) good-looking
2) best-company
3) famous
4) made a good living

And I wouldn't have traded him for anybody as so few people have so many of the desirabilities

They were married in the rectory of St Patrick's Cathedral in New York; Scott was a Catholic (lapsed) and Zelda, as yet, had no religious affiliation that mattered. "It will take more than the Pope to make Zelda good," her mother thought, but Scott had his princess and Zelda her route to "high places."

"Don't you think I was made for you?" she asked Scott. "I feel like you had me ordered — and I was delivered to you — to be worn — I want you to wear me like a watch-charm or a button-hole bouquet — to the world."

The question of who was made for whom, who did the ordering and who wore the charm, arose very early in the Fitzgeralds' marriage. "I'm absolutely nothing without you," Zelda insisted, " — Just the doll that I should have been born." She had no higher goal than "amusement," she said; she was "an extravagant," good for nothing but "useless, pleasure-giving pursuits." In a joint newspaper interview, Scott described his wife as "the most charming person in the world," then added: "That's all. I refuse to amplify — excepting she's perfect."

"You don't think that," Zelda replied. "You think I'm a lazy woman."

"No," said Scott. "I like it. I think you're perfect. You're always ready to listen to my manuscripts at any hour of day or night."

They were America's golden couple, the living embodiment of the "Roaring Twenties" and reckless progenitors of the Jazz Age. Scott named the age himself, while Zelda jumped in fountains, danced on tables, "showed her knees," and munched on chewing gum. She was probably the most famous "flapper" in America, but also the first to herald the flapper's demise: it was Zelda who pronounced the flapper "deceased" in a published "Eulogy" in 1922. "I am assuming that the Flapper will live by her accomplishments and not by her Flapping," she observed — she had as witty a turn of mind as any other in that era of memorable wisecracks. ("Did you ever see a woman's face with so many fine, large teeth in it?" Zelda asked on meeting a friend of Scott's.) In New York, Zelda and Scott had honeymooned at the Biltmore (where they were asked to leave when "the continued hilarity of their presence" began to disturb the other guests) and later at the Commodore (where they amused themselves by spinning endlessly in the revolving door and performing cartwheels in the lobby). Already they had begun a lifelong pattern of shopping, drinking, talking, collapsing, traveling, quarreling and "making it up." Edmund Wilson, a schoolmate of Scott's at Princeton, testified to the Fitzgeralds' amazing "capacity for carrying things off and carrying people away by their spontaneity, charm, and good looks. They had a genius for imaginative improvisations" and quickly found themselves adopted by the city's "smart set": H. L. Mencken, George Jean Nathan, Dorothy Parker. They were "the arch type of what New York wanted," Scott remembered, "We felt like small children in a great bright unexplored barn." Neither of the Fitzgeralds was in any doubt as to what they represented, of the need they served for glamour and excitement after the trauma of the First World War. "When Zelda Sayre and I were young," said Scott, "the war was in the sky." Their collected epigrams might fill a small book:

Scott: It was an age of miracles, it was an age of art, it was an age of excess, and it was an age of satire.

Zelda: We had a good time.

Scott: I was in love with a whirlwind.... She was perhaps the delicious, inexpressible, once-in-a-century blend.

Zelda: I hate a room without an open suitcase in it. It seems so permanent.

Scott: Liquor on my breath is sweet to her. I cherish her most extravagant hallucinations.

Zelda: I like men to be just incidents in books so I can imagine their characters.

Scott: If I had anything to do with creating the manners of the contemporary American girl I certainly made a botch of the job.

Zelda: Youth does not need friends — it needs only crowds.

Scott: Sometimes I don't know whether Zelda and I are real or whether we are characters in one of my novels.

Zelda: All I want is to be very young always and very irresponsible.

That Zelda was the model for many of Scott Fitzgerald's fictional heroines is not a point to be debated. It was no secret even at the time that he "used" Zelda and Zelda's experience in the interest of his art. Nor did Zelda appear to object to her role as muse, though this issue — who owned what — would later rise up as the most famous dispute between them. In 1922, when Scott published *The Beautiful and Damned*, Zelda remarked in a review for the *New York Tribune* that she had "recognized a portion of an old diary of mine" while reading the book, "and also scraps of letters which, though considerably edited, sound to me vaguely familiar." Mr Fitzgerald "seems to believe that plagiarism begins at home," said Zelda. Privately, she was proud, calling her husband "a prophet" and herself his willing disciple. "He endowed those years that might have been so garishly reckless with the dignity of his bright indicative scene," she wrote, "and buoyed the desperation of a bitter day."

"I never thought she was beautiful," said Dorothy Parker, one of Scott Fitzgerald's most adoring friends and admirers. "She was very blond with a candy box face and a little bow mouth, very much on a small scale and there was something petulant about her.... But they did both look as though they had just stepped out of the sun; their youth was striking." People noticed that they looked alike — that they might even have been brother and sister. The actress Louise Brooks saw the

Zelda's proposed book jacket for *The Beautiful and Damned*

Fitzgeralds in Hollywood in the late 1920s, "and the first thing that struck me," she wrote, "was how *small* they were." Brooks had come to meet "the genius writer, but what dominated the room was the blazing intelligence of Zelda's profile ... the profile of a witch." It had taken Scott's relations and friends a little time to get used to Zelda's tactics: she liked to receive their visitors while sitting in her bath, and confessed to

Edmund Wilson that the sight of a hotel room left her "erotically charged." She had a mesmerizing influence on everyone who met her, and a particular way of talking that no one who knew her forgot.

"She talked with so spontaneous a color and wit," said Wilson, " — almost exactly in the way she wrote — that I very soon ceased to be troubled by the fact that the conversation was in the nature of free association of ideas and one could never follow up anything. I have rarely known a woman who expressed herself so delightfully and so freshly; she had no ready-made phrases on the one hand and made no straining for effect on the other." Everyone knew, and believed, that Zelda could write, and if she didn't it was because, at this stage of things, she was too busy *living* her role to record it. In 1921 she had a baby, and remarked to Scott as she came out of the ether, "Oh God, goofo, I'm drunk."

The baby, "Scottie," was almost as famous as her parents in their time. "LILLIAN GISH IS IN MOURNING," Scott wired Zelda's parents when his daughter was born: "CONSTANCE TALMADGE IS A BACK NUMBER A SECOND MARY PICKFORD HAS ARRIVED." The Fitzgeralds were "expecting a boy," as the saying is, and their only child, perhaps in compensation, was christened Frances Scott Fitzgerald. For a number of years Zelda called her "Patricia" — a sign of the strangely disconnected manner she brought to the art of motherhood.

"The best flapper is reticent emotionally and courageous morally," Zelda explained. "You always know what she thinks, but she does her feeling alone." It was a kind of creed and an affirmation, immensely important, of a woman's right to her independence. Throughout the 1920s, and even more intensely after Scottie's birth, the Fitzgeralds moved in a world of grand hotels and fancy bars, summer cottages and trips abroad, "a world of nannies and beach umbrellas and *espadrilles*, of hot gusts filtering through closed shutters and faded cars cooking on driveways." If anything, motherhood had only heightened Zelda's aura of glamour, for the baby was as pretty as her parents and seemed born for a luxury ride. Even when they had no money the Fitzgeralds behaved (and were treated) as if they had. "We don't go in for self-preservation," they declared. "When we married we made up our minds never to be afraid." In 1922 they rented a house at Great Neck, on Long Island, where Scott began the work that became *The Great Gatsby* and Zelda matched him drink for drink. It was a "very alcoholic & chaotic" time, she remembered: "It was always tea-time or late at night." In 1930, in a rambling letter to Scott, Zelda recalled the nervous tenor of those days:

The strangeness and excitement of New York, of reporters and furry smothered hotel lobbies.... There were flowers and nightclubs ... absinthe cocktails ... and the road-house where we bought gin.... There were my white knickers that startled the Connecticut hills, and the swim in the sandalled lady's bird-pool. The beach, and dozens of men, mad rides along the Post Road and trips to New York. We never could have a room at a hotel at night we looked so young, so once we filled an empty suit case with the telephone directory and spoons and a pin-cushion at The Manhattan.... We quarreled and you broke the bathroom door and hurt my eye.... We trailed through Central Park in the snow after a ball at the Plaza.... We gave lots of parties.... We drank always and finally came to France because there were always too many people in the house.

The drinking was out of control well before the Fitzgeralds moved to Paris and joined (or helped to create) the "Lost Generation" of American writers and artists in France. As early as 1919 Zelda's parents had been worried about Scott's "imbibing" and wondered what their daughter was getting into. "Darling heart," Zelda wrote Scott at the time, " — I won't drink *any* if you object." But of course he didn't. Together they caused so many scenes and passed out so often at parties as to become a kind of national attraction. "Here come the Fitzgeralds!" their friends exclaimed when they entered a room; before the night was over Scott might well have busted up the furniture, tossed figs at his hostess, or chewed and swallowed a wad of twenty-dollar bills before crumpling to the floor.

"You can drink some of the cocktails all of the time and all of the cocktails some of the time, but — think it over, Judy," Scott wrote while inscribing a book for a friend. When asked why *she* drank so much, Zelda replied: "Because the world is chaos and when I drink

I'm chaotic." In 1923 the actress Laurette Taylor left a party at the Fitzgeralds' with the remark that she had "just seen the doom of youth. Understand? The doom of youth itself. A walking doom." Even now Zelda was showing incipient signs of the madness that later overtook her completely, riding to the theater on the hoods of cabs and hooting with laughter at the most solemn moments. "I have cat thoughts that chase the mice thoughts," she explained, "and sometimes they will get

Zelda, Scott, and Scottie in Rome · 1924

all the mouse thoughts caught and I read Aeschylus to put myself to sleep." One night on the French Riviera she nearly drove off the Grande Corniche with the declaration, "I think I'll turn off here," another time she lay down in front of their parked car and said, "Scott, drive over me." (Apparently he was ready to do so until sounder minds intervened.) Before they left New York for Paris Scott was sober enough to remark in his *Ledger* that their marital situation was "comfortable but dangerous and deteriorating. No ground beneath our feet." Zelda herself summed it all up in a novel she never finished:

There were many changing friends and the same old drinks and glamour and story swept their lives up into the dim vaults of lobbies and stations until, as one said, *évènements* accumulated. It might have been Nemesis incubating.

It was. "One day in 1926 we looked down and found we had flabby arms and a fat pot and couldn't say boop-boop-a-doop to a Sicilian," Scott wrote. "By 1927 a widespread neurosis began to be evident, faintly signaled, like a nervous beating of the feet." 1927 was the year Lindbergh crossed the ocean and Isadora Duncan strangled on her scarf. Not long before, when dining with Zelda at a restaurant in St Paul de Vence, Scott had been summoned to Isadora's table, where he sat at her feet for more than an hour while she clucked and cooed and rubbed her fingers through his thick blond hair. Neither seemed to notice when Zelda, fed up, literally flung herself down a flight of stone stairs and crashed into a door below. It was only one of the stranger manifestations of her mounting discontent. In Hollywood, not long after, when Scott began an earnest flirtation with the actress Lois Moran, Zelda burned her dresses in the bathtub and tossed away a diamond watch he had given her. The writer Rebecca West remembered that there was always something "frightening" about Zelda "not that one was frightened from one's own point of view," said West, "only from hers." Most of her photographs from this period depict her with a hard expression, as if she were permanently irritated, surprised by the camera and just waiting for the intruder to leave.

"Now, Ludlow," Zelda remarked to Ludlow Fowler, a friend of Scott's who had been best man at their wedding, "take it from an old souse like me — don't let drinking get you in the position it's gotten Scott if you want your marriage to be any good." She had had an "affair" almost as soon as they got to France, a tender but allegedly unconsummated romance with a French aviator, Edouard Jozan, whom she and Scott had met on the Riviera at the same time they met Gerald and Sara Murphy, the wealthy American aristocrats who were the undisputed leaders, the central focus, of

Ellerslie

expatriate life in France. Zelda's Jozan was strikingly handsome in the French manner, "full of the sun," as she remembered, with "the head of the gold of a Christmas coin" and "convex shoulders [that] were slim and strong." She had never stopped flirting with any man who caught her fancy, but this was something different. Long before she met Jozan, Zelda had warned Scott "that if he were away she could sleep with another man and it wouldn't really affect her, or make her really unfaithful to him." It was a claim, after all, that men had made for generations to their wives: for Zelda, sex appears to have been a fairly impersonal transcendent experience. Scott, meantime, according to his friends, was "not strongly sexed." He was angry enough in 1925 to banish Jozan from the house, and Zelda was upset enough to attempt suicide afterwards by swallowing a bottle of sleeping pills. Scott's blindness to her misery is best reflected in a comment from his *Ledger* after Jozan had gone: "Zelda and I close together. Trouble clearing away."

For the next five years, until Zelda's breakdown in Paris in 1930, the Fitzgeralds continued their life on the wing, sometimes in Europe, sometimes in the States, where they rented Ellerslie, a nineteenth-century mansion outside Wilmington, Delaware, and scaled new heights (or depths) of raucousness, dissipation, and marital discord. "There were four or five Zeldas and at least eight Scotts," said James Thurber, "so that their living room was forever tense with the presence of a dozen desperate personalities, even when they were alone in it." When it came to public appearances the Fitzgeralds were *all* of their characters equally. Scott declared it as his highest aspiration "to stay married and in love with Zelda and write the greatest novel in the world." Zelda, unfortunately, had no such external motivation to prevent her from going over the edge. In February

1925, just before the publication of *The Great Gatsby*, the Fitzgeralds had vacationed on the isle of Capri, and it was here, so far as anyone knows, that Zelda took her first painting lessons. She had always painted, as she had always danced; now, as the party her life had been staggered to its close, dancing became her reason for being. Later she insisted that she had begun to study the ballet in earnest, at the age of twenty-seven, only because she had "nothing to do." She had wanted "something of her own," she said, to "drive the devils that had driven her." In Paris, she studied with the Diaghilev *corps de ballet*, and took private lessons with Lubov Egorova, Diaghilev's director of dance. At the same time she was writing short stories, among them five that were sold to *College Humor* and one — "A Millionaire's Girl" — that appeared in the *Saturday Evening Post* under Scott's name in order to command a larger fee. It needs to be said in defense of them both that Scott was never insensitive to Zelda's multiple talents, nor ever unconscious of her very real achievement: when she broke down completely in 1930, he encouraged her to keep writing.

"I think you'll see that apart from the beauty and richness of the writing [Zelda's stories] have a strange haunting and evocative quality that is absolutely new," Scott wrote Max Perkins, his editor at Scribners in New York. "I think too that there is a certain unity apparent in them — their actual unity is a fact because each of them is the story of her life when things for a while seemed to have brought her to the edge of madness and despair." About Zelda's ballet lessons he was less enthusiastic.

"She no longer read or thought," he grumbled, "or knew anything or liked anyone except dancers and their cheap satellites. People respected her because I concealed her weaknesses, and because of a certain complete fearlessness and honesty that she has never lost, but she was becoming more and more an egotist and a bore." It was out of the question, of course, that Zelda would ever become a fully accomplished ballerina: she had begun her study too late for that. Nevertheless she was "proficient," and capable, in her teacher's opinion, of dancing featured roles with any company in the world. The judgment was just enough to keep her going — and keep her going mad.

"I began to like Egorova," she wrote Scott later on:

...I told you I was afraid there was something abnormal in the relationship and you laughed.... I began to work harder at dancing — I thought of nothing else but that. You were far away by then and I was alone.... I had my lesson in the afternoon and I walked at night.... You were constantly drunk. You didn't work and were dragged home at night by taxi-drivers when you came home at all. You said it was my fault for dancing all day. What was I to do?... I worked all the time.... I couldn't walk in the street unless I had been to my dancing lesson. I couldn't manage the apartment because I couldn't speak to the servants. I couldn't go into stores to buy clothes and my emotions became blindly involved.

A lot of people already believed that Zelda Fitzgerald was "crazy" — notably Ernest Hemingway, whom Scott himself had "discovered" in Paris and whom Zelda wrote off as "bogus ... a pansy with hair on his chest." They despised each other, and when Zelda was finally taken to a hospital outside Paris to be treated for "nervous exhaustion," she declared to the doctors that "her husband was a homosexual, in love with a man named Hemingway." Though she eventually apologized, the damage was done: nothing she ever said or did could have caused a greater rumpus.

"It's frightful," said Zelda as she entered the first of many sanatoriums.

...It's horrible, what's going to become of me, I must work and I no longer can, I must die and yet I have to work. I'll never be cured, let me go, I have to see Madame [Egorova], she has given me the greatest joy in the world, it's comparable to sunlight falling on a block of crystal, to a symphony of perfumes, to the most perfect strains of the greatest masters of music.

She had been drinking, and at first her doctors diagnosed her as a "petite anxieuse, worn out by her work in a milieu of professional dancers." Later, there was no concealing the grievous nature of Zelda's disease. Dr Paul Bleuler, an authority on schizophrenia who consulted on Zelda's case at a clinic in Prangins, near Geneva, described her as "a constitutional, emotionally unbalanced psychopath"; Zelda, in turn, regarded Dr Bleuler as "a great imbecile," and indeed, one of the most striking (and tragic) aspects of her battle with schizophrenia was the sheer lucidity she brought to bear on the problem. From Prangins, she wrote Scott:

I seem awfully queer to myself… but I know I used to have integrity even if it's gone now.… You've got to come and tell me how I was. Now I see odd things, people's arms too long or their faces as if they were stuffed and they look tiny and far away, or suddenly out of proportion.

Neither of the Fitzgeralds was prepared to admit that Zelda's illness was incurable. From time to time, she was visited by furious attacks of eczema, and Scott wondered if she was not merely the victim of some chemical imbalance. "I can't help clinging to the idea that some essential physical thing like salt or iron or semen or some unguessed at holy water is either missing or is present in too great quantity," he told Zelda's doctors. Scott was always mindful of the general opinion that he himself had driven Zelda to insanity, a view that Zelda, in her distress, was all too ready to encourage.

She wrote Scott in a stream of agitated letters from the clinic in Switzerland:

Try to understand that people are not always reasonable when the world is as unstable and vacillating as a sick head can render it — That for months I have been living in vaporous places peopled with one-dimensional figures and tremulous buildings until I can no longer tell an optical illusion from a reality — that head and ears incessantly throb and roads disappear, until finally I lost all control and powers of judgement and was semi-imbecilic when I arrived here.

Scott, not surprisingly, was inclined to blame Zelda's psychic breakdown on her family in Montgomery, in particular on her father, Judge Sayre, whose "overly rational" approach to life had clashed with Zelda's own "ebullient" nature; and on her mother, who had nursed her to the age of four — until she "could have chewed sticks," as Zelda said. In the meantime Scott refused to give up drinking for Zelda or anyone else.

"I cannot consider one pint of wine at the day's end as anything but one of the rights of man," he said. "Any human value I might have would disappear if I condemned myself to a life-long asceticism to which I am not adapted either by habit, temperament, or the circumstances of my metier." In 1932, after Zelda had first got better, and then got worse, Scott predicted that he would "probably be carried off eventually by four strong guards, shrieking manicly that after all I was right and she was wrong, while

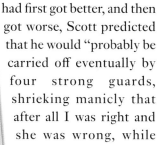

Zelda is followed home by an adoring crowd in an automobile banked with flowers, and offered a vaudeville contract." Zelda, for her part, had little doubt as to which of them was suffering more. She would live the rest of her days in and out of madness, at no point unaware of her own degeneration and the failure of her hopes.

Now that I can't sleep any- more I have lots to think about," she told Scott, *"and since I have gone so far alone I suppose I can go the rest of the way — but if it were Scot- tie I would not ask that she go through the same hell, and if I were God I could not justify a reason for imposing it.*

It was Scottie, in later years, whose love for them both helped redeem the image and the memory of the Fitzgeralds. Scottie remembered "a golden childhood" to the age of "about eleven," and after that, mainly in her father's company, "nothing but the troubles that were reflected in our relations — my mother's hopeless illness, his own bad health and lack of money, and, hardest of all, I think, his literary eclipse." These were the years of Scott's own breakdown, which he chronicled with hair-raising precision in the *Crack-Up* series. "Waste and horror" were the words he used to describe his decline, " — what I might have been and done that is lost, spent, gone, dissipated, unrecapturable." It is ever to his credit that Scott never turned his back on Zelda in her trouble, and that their daughter emerged from these devastating years with her dignity and identity intact. After the so-called second wave of American feminism, in the early 1970s, Zelda came more and more to be regarded as a put-upon and misunderstood figure, a creative genius mercilessly "squashed" and "squelched" by her husband in his jealousy.

Zelda in North Africa · 1930

"It's a script that reads well," Scottie observed, "and will probably remain a part of the 'Scott and Zelda' mythology forever, but is not, in my opinion, accurate.... It is my impression that my father greatly appreciated and encouraged his wife's unusual talents and ebullient imagination.... He did raise a terrible row when she published her novel.... But this sort of competition is traditionally the bane of literary romances."

The novel was Zelda's *Save Me the Waltz,* which she finished at the Phipps Psychiatric Clinic in Baltimore after her second breakdown in 1932. Her beautiful, weird book, plainly autobiographical and unsparing in its depiction of genius gone mad, was published by Scribners, Scott's own publisher, but not before Scott had demanded major changes in the text. He was finishing his own account of their adventures in *Tender Is the Night.*

"Turning up in a novel signed by my wife," he argued, "...puts me in an absurd & Zelda in a ridiculous position. This mixture of fact & fiction is calculated to ruin us both, or what is left of us, and I can't let it stand.... My God, my books made her a legend and her single intention in this somewhat thin portrait is to make me a non-entity." In vain Zelda protested that her work was "therapeutic," that the story of their lives belonged as much to her as to him: Scott was convinced she had "poached" his territory and stolen his fire. That neither *Save Me the Waltz* nor *Tender Is the Night* sold especially well when they first appeared can only have made things worse. From this fiasco date the harshest words that Scott is known to have hurled at his wife.

"You are a third-rate writer and a third-rate ballet dancer," he told Zelda during a famous "session" in her doctor's office.

"It seems to me that you are making a rather violent attack on a third-rate talent, then," she replied. Nevertheless she agreed to Scott's demands: she altered her text. She was not trying to be "a great artist or a great anything," she wrote Scott. It was not "the will-to-power" or any exaggerated ambition that drove her to create, but other "motivating elements." Without an outlet, she was without a self.

"It was my mother's misfortune to be born with the ability to write, to dance, *and* to paint," said Scottie, "and then never to have acquired the discipline to make her talent work for, rather than against, her." Zelda never stopped writing, and she never stopped dancing, but it was painting, after this, that took center stage. In 1934, she had an exhibition of her painting and drawings at the Cary Ross Gallery in New York. She wrote to Scott:

You talk of the function of art, I wonder if anybody has ever got nearer the truth than Aristotle: he said that all emotions and all experience were common property — that the transposition of these into form was individual and art.... It seems to me the artist's business is to take a willing mind and guide it to hope or despair contributing not his interpretations but a glimpse of his honestly earned scars of battle and his rewards.

In the wake of the lukewarm reception to *Tender Is the Night* she urged Scott not to "worry about critics — what sorrows have they to measure by, or what lilting happiness with which to compare those ecstatic passages?" Meantime life was not a contest, nor "an inexhaustible store of efforts to no deeper purpose than that of ameliorating the immediate circumstance." Their mutual devotion, strengthened and ennobled by terrible suffering, never really wavered:

Zelda: You are all I care about on earth — the past discredited and disowned, the future has doubled up on the present; give me the peace of my one certitude — that I love you.

Scott: I can carry most of contemporary literary opinion, liquidated, in the hollow of my hand — and I do, I see the swan floating on it and — I find it to be you and you only.

In a letter to Scottie in 1940, the year he died, Scott asked his daughter to "be sweet" to Zelda. The insane were merely "guests on earth," he said, "eternal strangers carrying around broken decalogues that they cannot read."

"I have asked a lot of my emotions," Scott reflected, " — one hundred and twenty stories. The price was high, right up with Kipling, because there was one little drop of something — not blood, not a tear, not my seed, but me more intimately than these, in every story, it was the extra I had." Here, in Zelda Fitzgerald's paintings, drawings, and fabulous paper dolls is the permanent complement to these words — the "extra" Zelda had and the record of her worth.

The dunes — Biskra

Looking for a mirage

Scott in North Africa · 1930

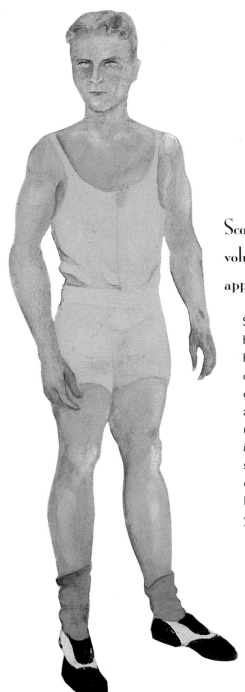

Early Paper Dolls

Scottie discussed the paper dolls in a foreword to Bits of Paradise, a volume of previously uncollected stories by Scott and Zelda that appeared in 1973:

Some of them represented the three of us. Once upon a time these dolls had wardrobes of which Rumpelstiltskin could be proud. My mother and I had dresses of pleated wallpaper, and one party frock of mine had ruffles of real lace cut from a Belgian handkerchief. More durable were the ball dresses of Mesdames de Maintenon and Pompadour....Perfectly preserved are the proud members of the courts of both Louis XIV and King Arthur (figures of haughty mien and aristocratic bearing), a jaunty Goldilocks, an *insouciant* Red Riding Hood, an Errol Flynn-like D'Artagnan, and other personages familiar to all little well-instructed boys and girls of that time. It is characteristic of my mother that these exquisite dolls, each one requiring hours of artistry, should have been created for the delectation of a six-year-old.

Scott's costumes · 10 1/2 in.

There seemed to be some heavenly support beneath his shoulder blades that lifted his feet from the ground in ecstatic suspension, as if he secretly enjoyed the ability to fly but was walking as a compromise to convention.

—*Save Me the Waltz* · 1932

Family

c. 1932
Courtesy of Cecilia L. Ross

These paper dolls were probably made at La Paix, in Towson, Maryland.

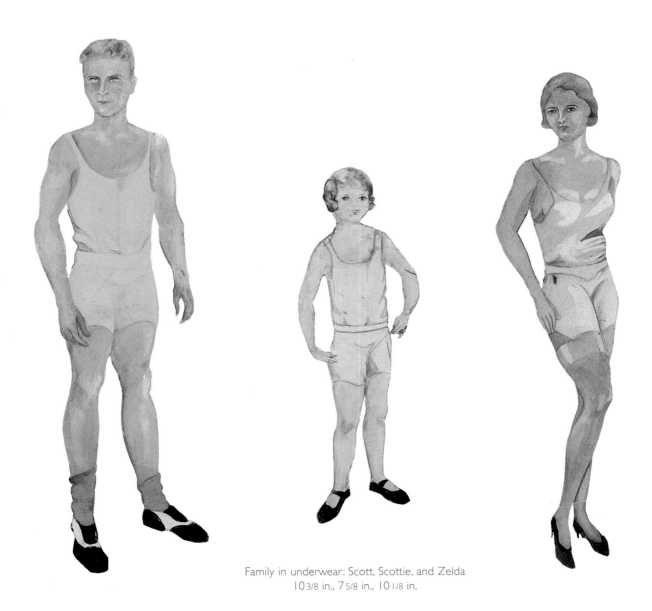

Family in underwear: Scott, Scottie, and Zelda
10 3/8 in., 7 5/8 in., 10 1/8 in.

Little Scottie · 7 1/8 in.

Big Scottie · 9 in.

Louis XIV

c. 1927
Courtesy of Eleanor Lanahan

Although Zelda painted numerous sets of paper dolls, the earliest one, the Louis XIV series, was probably painted for Scottie at Ellerslie in Delaware. (This selection from the Louis XIV series continues through page 39.)

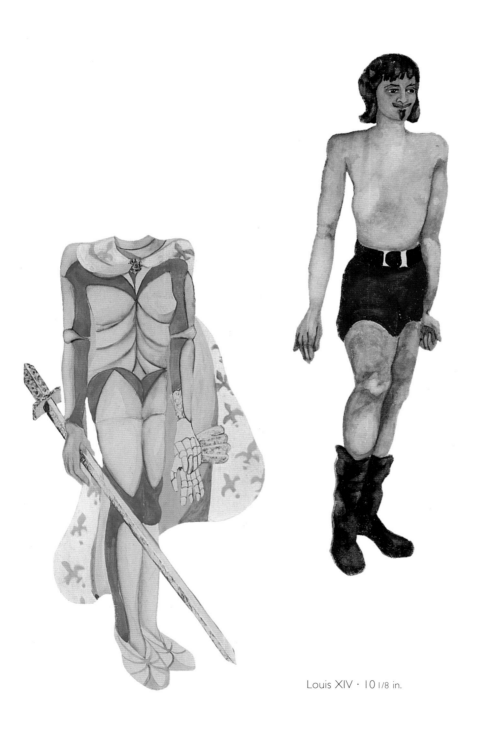

Louis XIV · 10 1/8 in.

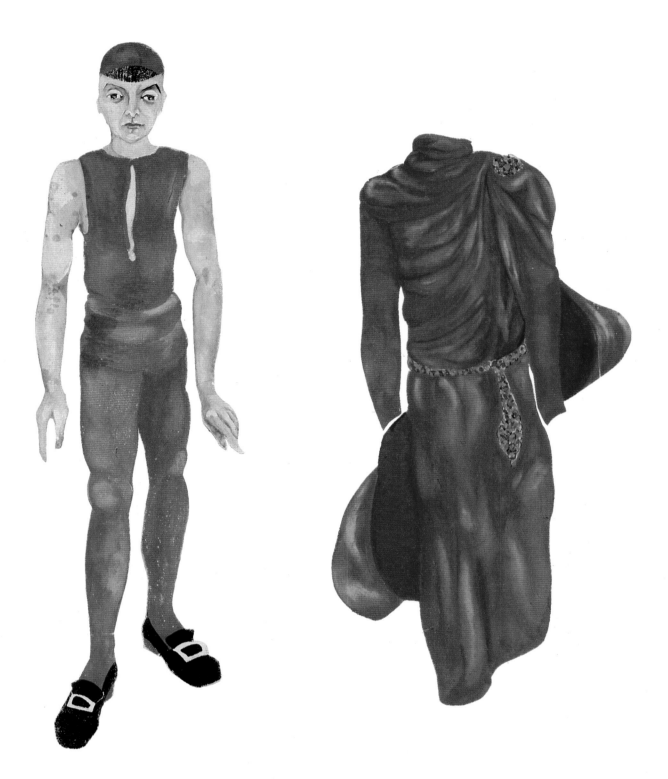

Cardinal Richelieu · 11 in.

11 1/2 in.

13 1/2 in.

Ladies of the court

12 in.

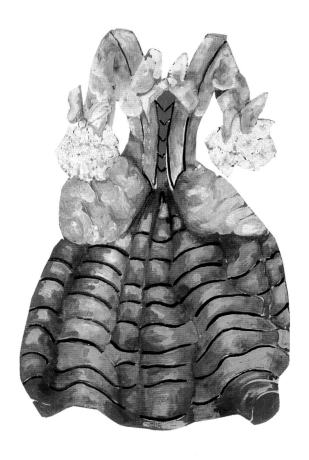

Ball gowns

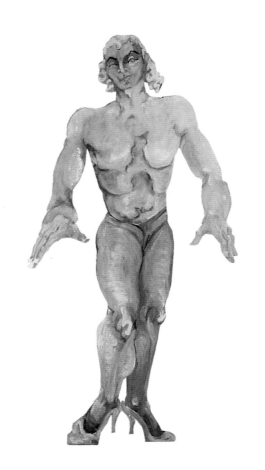

12 3/4 in.

12 3/4 in.

Courtiers

13 1/2 in.

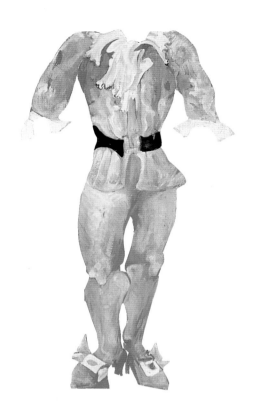

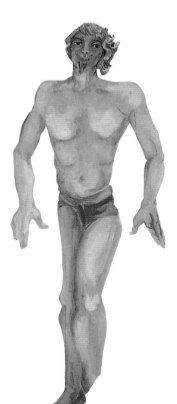

12 in.

Courtiers

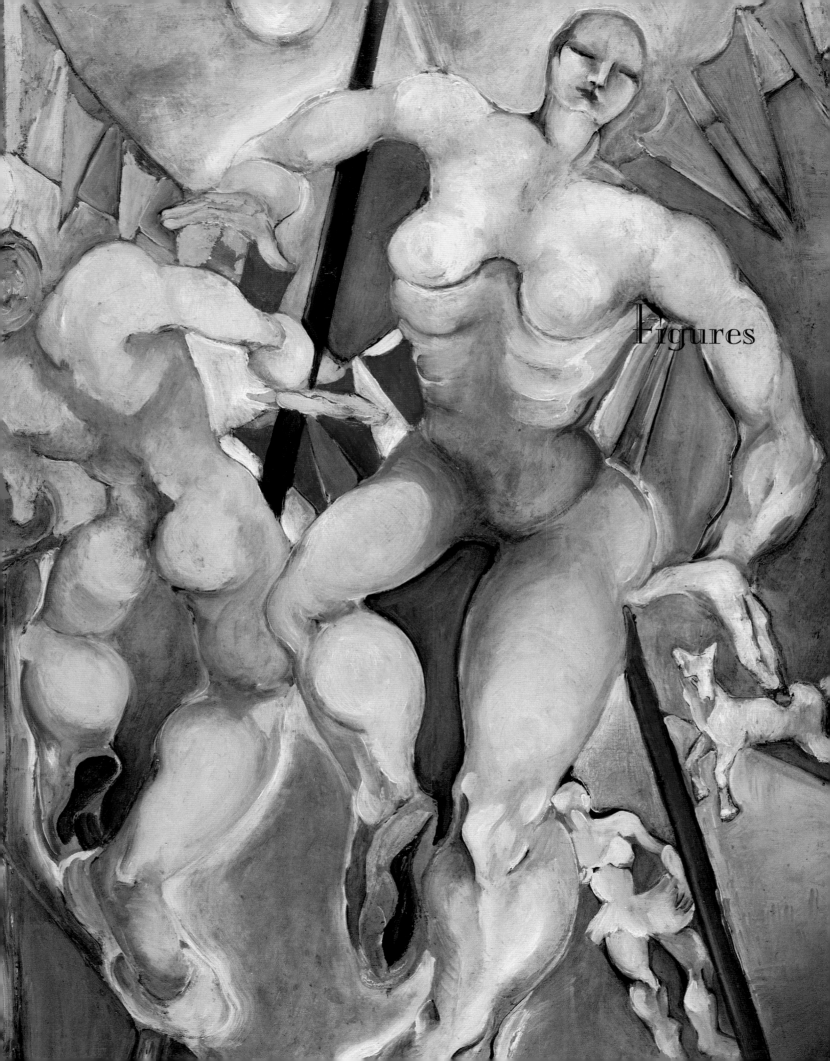

Figures

Self-Portrait

Early 1940s · Gouache on paper · 20 x 18 in.
*Courtesy of the Graphic Arts Collection, Visual Materials Division, Dept. of Rare Books and Special Collections,
Princeton University Libraries*

In 1942 Zelda exhibited a self-portrait, probably this one, at the Montgomery Museum of Fine Arts. A companion portrait of Scott has since disappeared. In "A Couple of Nuts," published in *Scribner's Magazine* in 1932, Zelda describes Lola:

> She was a protruding Irish beauty, full and carnivorous, with black hair slicking up her conical brows, and hunter's eyes that trapped and slew her mouth.

Opposite · Circus

c. 1942 · Oil on canvas · 35 1/2 x 23 1/2 in.
Courtesy of the Montgomery Museum of Fine Arts

Ballerinas Dressing

c. 1941 · Oil on canvas · 42 × 30 in.
Courtesy of Kristina Kalman Fares

In *Save Me the Waltz*, Zelda's autobiographical novel, she describes the internal sensation, rather than the appearance, of the rigors of ballet:

> Alabama's work grew more and more difficult. In the mazes of the masterful fouetté her legs felt like dangling hams; in the swift elevation of the entrechat cinq she thought her breasts hung like old English dugs. It did not show in the mirror. She was nothing but sinew. To succeed had become an obsession. She worked until she felt like a gored horse in the bullring, dragging its entrails.

Ballet Figures

c. 1941 · Oil on canvas · 35 1/2 x 25 1/2 in.
Courtesy of the Montgomery Museum of Fine Arts

This painting was shown at the American Art Association's Spring Salon in New York. On May 4, 1942, she gave it to the Montgomery Museum of Fine Arts.

> At night she sat in the window too tired to move, consumed by a longing to succeed as a dancer. It seemed to Alabama that, reaching her goal, she would drive the devils that had driven her — that, in proving herself, she would achieve that peace which she imagined went only in surety of one's self — that she would be able, through the medium of the dance, to command her emotions, to summon love or pity or happiness at will, having provided a channel through which they might flow. She drove herself mercilessly.

—Save Me the Waltz · 1932

Muscular Figure

Mid-1930s · Watercolor and gouache on grey paper · 25 x 19 1/2 in.
Courtesy of Roy and Janice Rudolph

Signed and dedicated bottom right: "With kindest regards to Mr. Crowninshield." Frank Crowninshield was the editor of *Vanity Fair* when it was owned by Condé Nast. Edmund Wilson, a Princeton classmate of Scott's, was also on the staff.

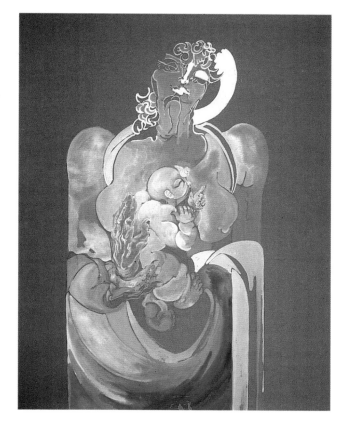

Nursing Mother with Blue Blanket

c. 1932–1934 · Gouache · 26 x 20 in.
Courtesy of the Johns Hopkins University

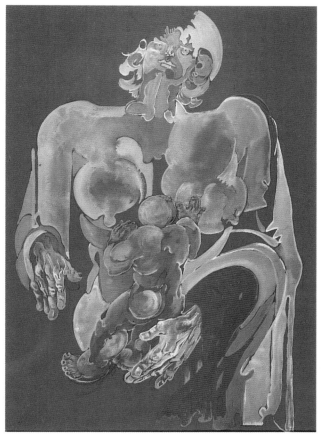

Nursing Mother with Red Blanket

c. 1932–1934 · Gouache · 24 x 18 1/4 in.
Courtesy of Kristina Kalman Fares

Bermuda Pad

These three sketches are from a pad Zelda took on a trip to Bermuda with Scott at the end of 1933. She had been discharged from the Phipps Clinic and was living as an outpatient in Baltimore. One month after their return, Zelda suffered her third breakdown. Of Bermuda, she wrote:

> The Elbow Beach Hotel was full of Honeymooners, who scintillated so persistently in each other's eyes that we cynically moved. The hotel St George was nice. Bougainvillea cascaded down the tree trunks and long stairs passed by deep mysteries taking place behind native windows… We drank sherry on a veranda above the bony backs of horses tethered in the public square. We had traveled a lot, we thought. Maybe this would be the last trip for a long while.
>
> —"Show Mr. and Mrs. F. to Room Number__" · 1934

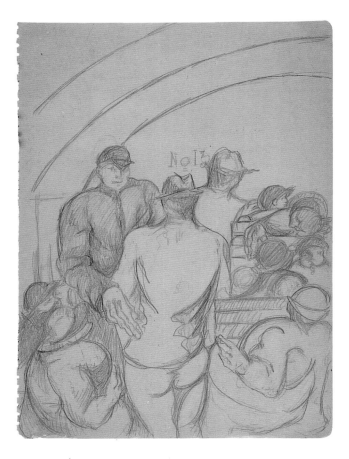

Figures on Bus

1933 · Pencil on paper · 14 1/2 x 10 1/2 in.
Courtesy of Eleanor Lanahan

Two Shipyard Workers

1933 · Pencil on paper · 14 1/2 x 10 1/2 in.
Courtesy of Eleanor Lanahan

Three Ballerinas

1933 · Pencil on paper · 14 1/2 × 10 1/2 in.
Courtesy of Eleanor Lanahan

After Scott's sudden death in 1940, Zelda produced a series of romantic cityscapes of New York and Paris.

Brooklyn Bridge

c. 1944 · Gouache on paper · 13 3/8 × 17 5/8 in.
Courtesy of Samuel J. Lanahan

Motoring home on summer evenings through the blue dusk that turns New York to a city under the sea, she would roll over the scalloped bridge hanging like draped lace between the stenographers and the families of American capitalists.

— "The Girl The Prince Liked" · 1930

Fifth Avenue

1940s · Gouache on paper · 13 5/8 × 17 1/2 in.
Courtesy of Cecilia L. Ross

Scott and Zelda were married in St Patrick's Cathedral on April 3, 1920. Scott's first novel and instant best-seller, *This Side of Paradise*, had been published one week earlier. This was the dawn of what he would term The Jazz Age — "the greatest, gaudiest spree in history." In this painting, a large, providential hand showers the crowd with theater tickets. Bouquets and top hats symbolize either participants in their wedding or in the Easter parade the following day.

Times Square

c. 1944 · Gouache on paper · 13 1/2 × 17 5/8
Courtesy of Samuel J. Lanahan

Twilights were wonderful just after the war. They hung above New York like indigo wash, forming themselves from asphalt dust and sooty shadows under the cornices and limp gusts of air exhaled from closing windows, to hang above the streets with all the mystery of white fog rising off a swamp. The faraway lights from buildings high in the sky burned hazily through the blue, like golden objects lost in deep grass, and the noise of hurrying streets took on that hushed quality of many footfalls in a huge stone square ...

—"The Millionaire's Girl" · 1930

Central Park

1940s · Gouache on paper · 13 3/4 x 17 3/4 in.
Courtesy of Cecilia L. Ross

Grant's Tomb

c. 1944 · Gouache on paper · 13 x 17 in.
Courtesy of Eleanor Lanahan

In a posthumous tribute to Scott, Zelda recalled that his fictional settings were always "the arena of some new philosophic offensive":

> The plush hush of the hotel lobby and the gala grandeur of the theater porte-cochère; fumes of orchidaceous elevators whirring to plaintive deaths the gilded aspirations of a valiant and protesting age, taxis slumberously afloat on deep summer nights—

> — "On F. Scott Fitzgerald" (published 1974)

Grand Central Station

c. 1943 · Gouache on paper · 13 3/4 × 17 3/4 in.
Courtesy of Cecilia L. Ross

Scottie and Jack Grand Central Time

c. 1943 · Gouache on paper · 13 3/4 x 17 3/4 in.
Courtesy of Cecilia L. Ross

When Ensign Jack Lanahan's ship arrived in the Brooklyn Navy Yard, in February 1943, he made a date to meet Scottie, "under the clock" of the Biltmore Hotel, one block from Grand Central station. "Within an hour he suggested that we get married," Scottie wrote, "something we had talked about before but always as in the future." The wedding was held a few days later. Zelda, unable to attend, commemorated the event with this painting of the couple's "timeless" romance.

Washington Square

c. 1944 · Gouache on paper · 13 5/8 x 18 1/4 in.
Courtesy of Cecilia L. Ross

After Scottie's wedding, Zelda wrote Harold Ober that New York was a "honey-moon mecca":

Giving Scottie away must have brought back the excitement of those days twenty-years ago when there was so much of everything adrift on the micaed spring time and so many aspirations afloat on the lethal twilights that one's greatest concern was which taxi to take and which magazine to sell to.

Notre Dame Cathedral

c. 1944 · Gouache on paper · 15 × 22 in.
Courtesy of Kristina Kalman Fares

This painting is dedicated to Xandra Kalman, wife of C. Oscar Kalman, friends of the Fitzgeralds from St Paul, Minnesota. Xandra and Zelda became friends when the Fitzgeralds moved to St Paul for Scottie's birth in 1921. In March 1930, the Kalmans visited the Fitzgeralds in Paris. Oscar Kalman was in a cab with Zelda, en route to her ballet class, when she had her first nervous collapse. He escorted her to Malmaison Clinic.

Place de l'Opera

c. 1944 · Gouache on paper · 13 × 17 in.
Courtesy of Eleanor Lanahan

I walked along with them under the dripping shadows of a Paris night, mauve and rose quartz under the streetlamps, pattery, clattery before the yellow cafés, droning, groaning, sucking its breath up the dark side streets…

That spring the lilacs dumped their skirts over the walls in the Boulevard St-Germain and wanderlust sprinkled the air. I wanted to stop at every "Rendezvous des Cochers" and "Paradis des Chauffeurs" I passed as I strolled along. It was like walking with a child beside you, the morning was so tender.

— "A Couple of Nuts" · 1932

The Pantheon and Luxembourg Gardens

c. 1944 · Gouache on paper · 14 3/4 x 21 1/8 in.
Courtesy of Eleanor Lanahan

I woke up one Sunday morning having lost my superiority on Saturday night and I thought it would make me feel more respectable to look at the cold equilibrium of the Luxembourg statues. So I did every surface thing a person can to myself and delivered my interior chimney-sweepishness onto the sidewalks. Symphonic taxi horns blew the muffled suppression of Sunday calmly through the narrow streets as I trod the quiet tones through the soles of my shoes.

— "A Couple of Nuts" · 1932

Arc de Triomphe

1940s · Gouache on paper · 15 x 22 in.
Courtesy of Mr & Mrs C. A. Kalman

In 1939, when Scottie returned from a summer in pre-war Europe, Zelda wrote:

I suppose that few people have seen more varied aspects of life at first hand than we did; known more different kinds of people or participated in more compelling destinies… Your generation is the last to bear witness to the grace and gala of those days of the doctrine of free will. I am so glad that you saw where the premium lay and savoured its properties before the end.

Madeleine Aperitifs

1940s · Watercolor on paper · 12 1/2 × 17 in.
Courtesy of the Scott & Zelda Fitzgerald Museum, Montgomery, Alabama

In 1931 Zelda wrote Scott from Prangins Clinic in Switzerland:

> *Was it fun in Paris? Who did you see there and was the Madeleine pink at five o'clock and did the fountains fall with hollow delicacy into the framing of space in the Place de la Concorde, and did the blue creep out from behind the Colonades of the rue de Rivoli through the grill of the Tuileries and was the Louvre gray and metallic in the sun and did the trees hang brooding over the cafés and were there lights at night and the click of saucers and the auto horns that play de Bussey—*

Landscapes

In 1936 Zelda transferred to Highland Hospital in Asheville, North Carolina. Her treatment included vigorous exercise — often a daily hike in the mountains. She blossomed in North Carolina and thrived on the area's natural beauty.

North Carolina Landscape

c. 1945 · Gouache on paper · 8 1/2 x 11 3/8 in.
Courtesy of the Montgomery Museum of Fine Arts

Candler, North Carolina

c. 1945 · Gouache on paper · 8 1/2 × 11 1/4 in.
Courtesy of the Montgomery Museum of Fine Arts

Hospital Slope

c. 1947 · Gouache on paper · 12 × 9 in.
Courtesy of the Wilson Library, University of North Carolina, Chapel Hill

Great Smoky Mountains

1940s · Gouache on paper · 9 x 11 1/2 in.
Courtesy of Eleanor Lanahan

In February 1935, Scott moved to North Carolina for his health. Zelda, a patient at Sheppard-Pratt Hospital in Baltimore, wrote to him of summers spent there in her youth:

> *North Carolina should be pines and pebbles, geraniums and red tile roofs — and very concise. Breathe in the blue skies. It's a good place to get up early; there's a very polished sun to burnish the mountain laurel before breakfast. And the books gleam cold in the thin early shadows. Biscuits and grits all floating in butter; resin on your hands and frogs bouncing out of the twilight.*

Mountain Landscape

c. 1947 · Watercolor on paper · 9 x 12 in.
Courtesy of Dr and Mrs Charles Graffeo

Soon after Zelda's death in 1948, the Sayre family cleaned out her studio and held a lawn sale. Louise Brooks, a Montgomery art dealer, discovered a three-foot stack of Zelda's oils. "I want the yard man to burn them," Zelda's sister told her, "I don't want them to be seen." Brooks succeeded in purchasing several sketchbooks and one oil — the one on top. When she returned the next day, the rest had been burned. This is one of the watercolors rescued by Brooks.

Flowers

Morning Glories

Undated · Gouache on paper · 11 x 9 1/2 in.
Courtesy of the family of Lillian Gish

Opposite · Chrysanthemums

Undated · Gouache on paper · 15 3/8 x 11 1/2 in.
Courtesy of Eleanor Lanahan

Calla Lilies

1940s · Gouache on paper · 20 1/4 x 12 3/4 in.
Courtesy of Charles Eric Kalman

At Highland Hospital, where gardening was part of her daily regimen, Zelda kept a notebook of sketches and thoughts. In one entry, she equates emotions with color. Aspiration, she noted, might be pale orchid, anchored with passion (vermillion.) Another page reads:

My lilies died; they just plain died and so I can only maybe paint the memory of white desirability of so much beauty. So perfect. I used to gather them in Alabama under the pines and from the ooze of a dried lake bed and they were always so spiritually splendid.

Wine and Roses

Undated · Gouache on paper · 31 × 25 in.
Courtesy of an anonymous lender

Hope

c. 1938 · Oil on canvas · 35 1/2 x 23 9/16 in.
Courtesy of the Montgomery Museum of Fine Arts

Sara Mayfield, Zelda's childhood friend and author of her biography, *Exiles in Paradise*, writes that this painting was "a dreamy study in which the cotton bolls resembled soft, blue bubbles she entitled 'Hope' to suggest a planter's vision of the harvest."

Still Life with Flowers

Undated · Oil on canvas · 30 × 24 in.
Courtesy of Mary Bear Norman

Mediterranean Midi

Undated · Oil on canvas · 44 × 40 in.
Courtesy of Mr & Mrs Charles Crommelin Nicrosi

Although the landscape is suggestive of Capri where Zelda, in 1925, is reported to have taken her earliest painting lesson, this painting probably dates from the 1940s.

On the Art of Zelda Fitzgerald

Jane S. Livingston

Parfois La Folie Est La Sagesse (*Sometimes Madness Is Wisdom*)

—The title Zelda chose for the catalogue of her exhibition
at the Cary Ross Gallery in Manhattan.

The irreducible impression presented by the artist Zelda Fitzgerald is that she was a natural — as writer, as athlete/dancer, and as illustrative artist. In the writing category, we have plenty of evidence of her innate gifts, with her best-known work, the novel *Save Me the Waltz*; and, even better, such blithe and unashamed autobiographical pieces as "A Couple of Nuts" and "Show Mr. and Mrs. F. to Number __", all written between 1930 and 1934. The air that Zelda's earlier prose often created, of issuing from a delightfully spoiled brat, is distilled in the following piece, published in 1925 in *Recipes of Famous Women*:

> Breakfast. See if there is any bacon, and if there is, ask the cook which pan to fry it in. Then ask if there are any eggs, and if so try and persuade the cook to poach two of them. It is better not to attempt toast, as it burns very easily. Also in the case of bacon, do not turn the fire too high, or you will have to get out of the house for a week....[1]

Striking a very different note — this time plangent, indeed heartbreaking — in 1931 Zelda wrote an elegant story that may be her most underrated, called "Miss Ella." Its ending lines eerily foreshadow the author's own final years, when she was living with her mother in Montgomery:

> Years passed but Miss Ella had no more hope for love. She fixed her hair more lightly about her head and every year her white skirts and peek-a-boo waists were more stiffly starched. She drove with Auntie Ella in

the afternoons, took an interest in the tiny church, and all the time the rims about her eyes grew redder and redder, like those of a person leaning over a hot fire, but she was not a kitchen sort of person, withal.[2]

Obviously, less direct evidence exists of Zelda's accomplishments as a dancer. But there are several recorded observations of various friends of the Fitzgeralds, and the evidence of her teachers' commitment — she studied intensively with Catherine Littlefield, director of the Philadelphia Opera Ballet Corps, and later with Littlefield's own teacher, Diaghilev's dance director, Madame Lubov Egorova. Many were struck by Zelda's athleticism, and how quickly she mastered balletic technique. Gerald Murphy's description of Zelda dancing in Egorova's Paris studio provides an especially compelling image of this strong-bodied woman at her *barre*: "grotesque in her intensity — one could see the muscles individually stretch and pull; her legs looked muscular and ugly..."[3] Though she had studied ballet as a child, Zelda began the serious study of ballet at the advanced age of twenty-seven, and achieved enough so that within three years she was invited to perform in a solo role with the Italian San Carlo Opera Ballet Company. She declined.

As a painter, Zelda left behind a concrete legacy that gains in stature with increased familiarity. What remains physically of both her whimsical, illustrational work, and the more solemn attempts at oil painting, represents only a part of her total production, since much may have been destroyed on March 10, 1948, in

Zelda at Salies-de-Beárn, 1926, with what appears to be a painting of Scott

the fire at the mental hospital in Highland, North Carolina that took Zelda's life. This was not the first fire: in June of 1933, a fire accidentally set by Zelda destroyed work at La Paix, the house near Baltimore where she and Scott were living in order to be near Johns Hopkins' Phipps Clinic, where she was receiving psychiatric treatment. And after Zelda's death, one of her sisters apparently ordered a group of her paintings burned. One suspects that even more of her own visual production might have been destroyed by the artist along the way.[4]

But based on much of what remains, fragmentary though it may be, the overwhelming impression is that Zelda Fitzgerald had a kind of supernally *innate*, and fecund, giftedness. From this recognition inevitably follows a sense of unconsummation. Yet in truth it is less remarkable that this complex woman's efforts produced an odd series of seemingly incomplete, or foreshortened bodies of work, than that so much was accomplished. Nor is it surprising that, given the attenuated nature of her creative energies, the most satisfying of the visual work is the essentially decorative, or illustrative, rather than the more deliberately "serious" paintings.

One of the several striking elements of Zelda Fitzgerald's rather untamed expressive life, is its brevity. Everything seemed to come to fruition at once, within a period of about five years (1929–1934), and then to reemerge sporadically for another handful of years before her death in 1948, at the age of forty-eight. The peculiar compression of this artistic burgeoning is made even more extraordinary by the fact that the years of her greatest discipline — as writer, dancer, and visual artist — coincided with the years when she was first hospitalized for and diagnosed with schizophrenia. Of the three outlets her creativity took, only in painting did Zelda Fitzgerald continue successfully to refine her art in the years following that dazzling initial outpouring.

Zelda's career as a writer of a few pieces of nonfiction, a dozen or so short stories, at least one play, and one novel, is now relatively well-known and fairly appreciated. This has not always been the case. Most early accounts of her contributions, and conflicts, as a writer centered on them in the context of her relationship with

La Paix

her famous husband. There is ample evidence to substantiate both private and overt rivalries between the two in the matter of Zelda's published writings, including the practice of certain magazine editors of putting Scott Fitzgerald's byline on her work, presumably with Scott's (and worse, Zelda's) consent, in order to sell more copies. Perhaps it is even more apropos to her periodic return to painting, that Scott occasionally lashed out at his wife, accusing her of co-opting *his* own subject matter — i.e., their shared experiences — in her writing.

Recently, however, greater attention has been given to Zelda's independent contribution as a writer of fiction and drama, notably with the 1991 publication of her collected writings, edited by Matthew J. Bruccoli. Pains have been taken to separate the texts clearly authored by Zelda and those done somehow "collaboratively" with Scott — and it is now possible to glean the full measure of Zelda's own distinctive prose style. Moreover, with respect to Zelda's actual attainment as a dancer, one only need reflect upon the school in which she was trained. Zelda plunged herself into the center of the most lastingly influential and demanding dance milieu of our time — that of Sergey Diaghilev, catalyst for the great coming together of Russian Classical Ballet and Parisian avant-garde values. She seems to have mastered the fundaments of its technique and, perhaps even more surprisingly, to have assimilated the style, or ethos, of this complex aesthetic.

The element of Zelda Fitzgerald's creative life that has not been seriously addressed — what in fact has been systematically ignored, even rejected, as a serious subject for evaluation and analysis — is her visual work. And while it seems clear that this aspect of her creativity is not altogether independent of, or separable from, her efforts in writing and ballet, neither is it merely a compensatory nor ancillary phenomenon.[5]

Interestingly, the few attempts that have been made to analyze or evaluate Zelda's visual art have resulted in a fundamentally misplaced emphasis on its relatedness to the *modernist* artists with whom she and Scott associated in Paris during the 1920s. On closer examination, we shall see that her best painting belongs securely in a rather conservative, even anti-modernist tradition. Among the artists of the day, her work resonates with American artists such as Thomas Hart Benton, Charles Demuth or the early Stuart Davis, to a much greater degree than with the European modernists. And to a still greater degree, much of the most interesting of Zelda's art belongs to the other culture she loved and understood — that of France. She was directly influenced by a certain strain of French illustrational art of the nineteenth and early twentieth centuries.

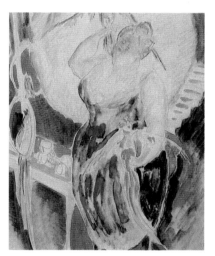

Bird Woman
Charles Demuth · 1917

Although we have only part of her total artistic output by which to judge, it is clear not only that Zelda had considerable facility in the medium of combined watercolor, pastel and gouache on paper, but that she worked with enormous discipline and purpose toward the end of mastering this technique. And we know that by the late 1930s, she conceived of herself as a professional artist. It may be that, at least in part, or at certain stages in her career, Zelda Fitzgerald held the opinion that we, her latter-day critics, have come to share: namely, that her best work is that done on paper, or in a frankly illustrative spirit, rather than what she created with oil on canvas. Zelda clearly worked hard at mastering the latter medium, but she was an astute critic of her own work, and may have felt, as we do viewing much of what is left of her paintings today, that her gifts flourished in smaller scale, and with ideas grounded in her love of fantasy subjects, especially myths, fairy tales, and memories.

As for her views of her own powers and preparedness as an artist, Zelda was both proud and defensive. In her biography of Zelda Fitzgerald, Nancy Milford relates that Zelda's attending physician at Highland Hospital in Asheville, Dr Robert Carroll, offered to pay her to paint floral designs on screens to be installed in a new hospital auditorium. Zelda wrote to her husband describing her reaction to this:

I sent word that I ultimately would not subscribe to the commandeering of a professional talent. The fact that an artist is temporarily incapacitated ought not to make him fair game to anybody who is able. My talent has cost a lot in heartache and paint-bills; and I don't want to compromise myself on such a major project that will make it difficult to get away, should such opportunity arise. To waste a professional talent, the cumulate result of years of effort, aspiration and heartbreak in a venture which will never see the light of day but most probably will be maltreated by every manifestation of psychosis is, to me, an abuse of the soul, human faith, and metier that is almost beyond my capacity to envisage.[6]

Zelda Fitzgerald's artistic production divides into several categories, identified by subject and type rather than by chronology. Since she rarely, if ever, dated or titled her works, it is difficult to know precisely when most of them were made. And there is in this body of work a peculiar lack of the usual stylistic "progression," or evolution, by which art historians often date and categorize an artist's works.

From the beginning, Zelda seemed determined to take on that most difficult of the draftsman's challenges, the human figure. She tried her hand at portraiture, achieving what are described as at least two excellent likenesses of her husband, which have disappeared, and more than one arresting self-portrait. A repeated theme in her work deals with generic figures, often dancers, approached not so much in the spirit of portraiture, or with an end to narrative expression, as in the cause of mastering the task of rendering them. These works occur in various media, ranging from pencil or charcoal on paper to oil on canvas. A few of these pieces, such as *Ballet Figures*, c. 1941 (right), occupy a place among the artist's first ranking works.

The congruences in Zelda's visual art with her life in dance on the one hand, and her verbal imagination on the other, occur in several ways. First, of course, is the recurrent subject of the dancer in her painting. One of the hallmarks of her figures, whether or not they are literally evoking a dancer's position, is their idiosyncratic, quasi-mannerist elongation of limb, and enlargement of the feet and hands. The artist supposedly addressed her own feeling about this habit of representation in a reply to the question, "Why do you paint all your characters with exaggerated limbs?" by saying, "Because that's how a ballet dancer feels after dancing."[7]

Ballet Figures
c. 1941

But of course the importance of such a repeated figural quirk is more complex, and grounded in more than the author's subjective interpretation. One of the keys to what truly attracted Zelda in other art, is found in these figures. Her distortion of the extremities has more than once been compared to Picasso's distortion of the figure. In fact, Zelda's distortions are much closer to a certain kind of illustrational (and essentially rather conservative) style of the time. Her style associates more with American artists such as Thomas Hart Benton, Reginald Marsh, and Paul Cadmus, than with the modernist artists with whom others have associated her.

Each of these artists, and some of the popular illustrators of the time such as Maxfield Parrish or Arthur Rackham, occasionally used the graphic device of distorting parts of the human figure — head, arms, legs — in the service of dramatic characterization. Though these artists seldom exaggerated the body's proportions to quite the degree that Zelda often did, like her they understood and deliberately used the device of exaggerating the feet, and sometimes the arms and hands, of their characters. Aside from the illusionistic power of this technique to emphasize the amount of physical space inhabited by the body, and of the gravitational pull being exerted on it, proportional shifts lend various overtones of psychological weight or levity to the figure. Not only in the dancing figures, but in virtually all of Zelda's fairy-tale creatures, this technique is used with great sophistication.

Because of her exposure to the set design of Diaghilev's ballet, Zelda has been compared to Mikhail Larionov, Natalie Goncharova and Léon Bakst; and because she knew them, she has been said to have been influenced by Picasso, Miró, Gris, or Matisse. She did indeed know most of these figures and their work very well, often seeing them in privileged circumstances. She visited the Gertrude Stein salon in Paris on more than one occasion, and is known to have devoured exhibitions of, and books about, the modernist painters in whose milieu she and Scott found themselves in both Europe and New York. And the influence of Gerald Murphy, both as painter and aesthete, cannot have left Zelda unmarked. Yet her own work is much more deeply connected to a markedly different tradition than the one with which most would have her identified.

A second subject running through her entire productive life is flowers. She reportedly depicted roses, violets, lilies, tulips, rhododendrons, poppies, Japanese magnolias, morning glories, orchids, hollyhocks, anemones, dahlias, and bachelor's buttons, among others.[8] Of all the commentary on Zelda's visual art in relation to her emotional illness, perhaps most has been made of the various psychological overtones found in the floral pictures (pp 70–75). According to most descriptions, Zelda's vocabulary in these pictures would appear to be dominated by images ranging from fetal unfurlings to phallic extrusions, rendered in a palette evoking either the febrile or necrophiliac. Aside from taking note of her lifelong fascination with flowers, and her frequent depiction of them, however, the floral paintings seem to me most noteworthy in relation to her professed fascination with Georgia O'Keeffe, and to underscore the essentially literal, or mimetic, impulse that moved Zelda to explore the subject time and again.

Beginning in the late 1930s, and continuing until her death, Zelda painted a number of scenes from the Bible (pp 114–121). These works are generally associated with her sudden and fervent embracing of Christianity starting in 1936, when she began to experience religious hallucinations as a result of her mental illness. Most of these paintings, however, were probably done in the late 1940s. Of all the types of work Zelda Fitzgerald made over her lifetime, the biblical allegories most literally express the anxieties and the psychological dislocations attaching to her fragile emotional state. A few of these paintings display a quality bordering on magnificence, by virtue of the sheer doggedness of their optical effect — their luminosity is often layered, seldom predictable — and for the ambitiousness of their narrative conception. Many

Mid-Manhattan # 1
John Marin · 1932

of them are invaded by a persistent aura of formulaic stiffness. In a manner completely unlike the spirit informing the best of her cityscapes, or the handful of idyllic North Carolina landscapes done at the same time, the religious works betray a tremendous effortfulness. Zelda's biblical subjects range from Old Testament narratives, including didactic pieces attempting to interpret the Commandments, to the classical episodes of Christ's nativity, miracles and martyrdom. Most of these paintings' labored atmosphere resides in their maker's transparent attempts to persuade others, or herself, of some ineffable truth. Through their quality of futilely attempted communication, the religious paintings assume a hard-won, if sadly compromised, dignity — always tempered by inadvertent twists of self-revelation. They are more objects for study than for delectation.

Around 1944, Zelda made a cycle of paintings, usually in watercolor and gouache on paper, depicting scenes from her long-ago travels with her husband and young child. These paintings, essentially a series of fanciful cityscapes of Paris and New York (pp 48–61), engaged some of the artist's most piquant imaginative faculties. Their subjects — Grant's Tomb, Washington Square, Arc de Triomphe, Place de l'Opera, etc. — are, on their face, fondly remembered landmarks commemorating the carefree days of Zelda's marriage to Scott. Yet rather than casually describing places remembered, they meditate on — and romanticize — their author's life in particular times and circumstances.

Region of the Brooklyn Bridge Fantasy
John Marin · 1932

These playful paintings both celebrate the past, and introduce elements of latter-day revisionism. They employ a distinctive palette, much different from the high-pitched one of her later renderings of scenes from Lewis Carroll's *Alice's Adventures in Wonderland* and other fairy-tale paintings. The imagined scenes from Zelda's younger days in New York are executed in a low-keyed color vocabulary, employing silvery greys judiciously counterbalanced with chalky salmons,

employ what amounts fundamentally to the construct of the theatrical stage, with its variable backdrops or sightlines or scrims, and its tricks on the theme of "Renaissance perspective." In these pictures, even more than in the children's illustrations, Zelda allows herself great freedom of invention in arranging objects and events, while retaining a legible overall compass. One is reminded of some of Charles Demuth's or John Marin's quasi-cubist compositions (p 81), especially those seemingly held together by sheer centrifugal force.

One summer day, when she was thirteen years old, she heard a voice at midday in her father's garden. A great light shone upon her, and the archangel St. Michael appeared to her. He told her to be a good girl and to go to church. Then, telling her of the great mercy which was in store for the Kingdom of France, he announced to her that she should go to the help of the Dauphin and bring him to be crowned at Rheims. " I am only a poor girl, " she said. " God will help thee, " answered the archangel. And the child, overcome, was left weeping.

Joan of Arc and the archangel St Michael from *Joan of Arc* by M. Boutet de Monvel

Much of Zelda's best work was done with the excuse of entertaining and educating her daughter, Scottie. Seldom has a child of an unsung artist received such a rich parental artistic legacy. At age seven, Scottie — living at Ellerslie, their grand house near Wilmington, Delaware — was presented with a still more majestic dollhouse, which "[Zelda] built herself, papering and painting it until it looked like a palace with elegant pieces of furniture and mirrors and glass windows,"[9] as well as an elaborately designed lampshade (pp 2–3), representing details of houses lived in, or places visited, in the United States and Europe.

or yellows, or blues. The emotional atmosphere of these chromatically muted pictures, far from being subdued or melancholy, is like the heightened sensation of an intense dream. Anchoring, or undergirding, these high-flying experiments in unconventional palette and surreal imagery, are their commandingly structured compositions. Here, at last, the artist has entirely mastered a synthesis between the illusion of a comfortably readable landscape arena, and a kind of densely occupied, fictional proscenium space. Nothing is quite literally disposed in these amusing cityscapes. They

visited, in the United States and Europe.

From the mid 1920s onward, Zelda saw to it that Scottie had her own, custom-made paper dolls and storytelling pictures. Her bed was painted with red and white stripes, and the walls of her bedroom were covered with scenes from children's stories. Later, in the 1940s, Zelda returned to many of these tales she and her young daughter read together, such as *Alice's Adventures in Wonderland*, interpreting them in forms — it is safe to say — unsurpassed by other illustrations of this classic work. Characters from Charles Perrault's Mother

Goose tales, the Brothers Grimm and the legend of King Arthur appear and reappear in the imagery Zelda created in this later artistic period. She seemed to be revisiting the stories shared years before with her daughter, now thinking of the grandchildren she would hardly know. Far from being a minor part of the lifework of Zelda Fitzgerald, this work constitutes the core of the production, both in terms of quantity and quality. An inescapable question — why Zelda never produced an illustrated children's book of her own — is partly answered in a letter she wrote to the publisher Maxwell Perkins inquiring about the possibility of producing a book of her paper dolls: "I have painted ... King Arthur's round-table. Jeanne d'Arc and coterie, Louis XIV and court, Robin Hood are under way. The dolls are charming.... Would you be kind enough to advise me what publishers handle such 'literature,' and how to approach?"[10] Perkins apparently saw the possibilities inherent in this impulse, and encouraged it. So we know that Zelda wished to publish her work, and, more important, to combine her verbal and pictorial talents. But finally the exigencies of simply functioning at a level to sustain the practice of her art, were as much as she was able to handle.

Joan of Arc
by M. Boutet de Monvel · 1896

One of the most enduringly satisfying results of Zelda's years of studying the human figure would emerge in an area some might think trivial, and that others of us may regard as culminative: the depth and authority the artist brings to her many variations on paper dolls and their costumes. Though it may be impossible to reconstruct the progression of her doll maquettes and the many costumes designed for each, it seems logical that the ones made in the 1940s for her grandchildren, have an anatomical verisimilitude, a sense of muscularity and truth of stance and balance, that probably developed from an earlier approach closer to the kind of stiff, generalized maquettes typical of most paper dolls. (It is known that a great quantity of dolls and costumes made for Scottie in her young childhood, as well as dollhouses and other objects, no longer exist.)

In addition to their striking vitality and anatomical accuracy, Zelda's paper dolls, particularly a series she made illustrating *The Three Musketeers* (p 109), evince another quality that sets them apart from other works in their genre, and relates them to some of her paintings. Their gender is sometimes barely identifiable. Males and females alike are heavily muscled, with exaggerated shoulders and torsos, slim waists swelling into powerful thighs, enlarged calves and the familiar oversized feet. The artist signals the femininity of her characters with rather formulaic features — ladylike hairdos, spherical breasts, and occasionally upturned chins. The men, in turn, sometimes display startlingly effeminate attributes: one musketeer has ruby lips and rouged cheeks. Others have wavy locks, and stand with their feet in a distinctly balletic position. The entire androgynous cast of Zelda's musketeers tableau is costumed in highly decorative fashion, taking full advantage of the trappings and flourishes with which members of both sexes dressed on Alexendre Dumas's imagined eighteenth-century stage. And it wasn't only within the chivalrous world of Dumas that Zelda endowed her male dolls with womanly accessories: their costumes often include lavish robes and ballet sandals. Papa Bear's wardrobe includes a skirt and slippers.

The preparation for Zelda's prolonged excursion into children's, or fantastically inspired, art, was based in two avenues of study. One was in reading the texts themselves. Zelda must have known the chivalrous literature of King Arthur's court virtually by heart, and her attention to the anecdotal niceties of the anthropomorphic fairy tales betrays a similar familiarity with those stories. The second source for her expertise in depicting and interpreting these fantasies came from a far more esoteric source: handbooks illustrating the costumes and accessories of successive historical eras.

From *L'Histoire du Costume Feminin Français*

Perhaps Zelda Fitzgerald's single favorite illustrative artist was the French artist, Maurice Boutet de Monvel. Among the books in Scottie's library was a copy of Boutet de Monvel's *Joan of Arc*, published by The Century Company of New York in 1923. Although the reproductions in this book are relatively pallid, and bear only a distant resemblance to the style of Zelda's illustrational work, the spirit in which Boutet de Monvel chose to depict scenes from the story of the martyred saint reminds one of the rather free and inventive approach Zelda took to her stories.

Far more revealing about Zelda's actual artistic source material for her children's illustrations, particularly in relation to the paper dolls, is another book Scottie passed on to her own daughter, Eleanor Lanahan. This

is a superbly produced volume titled *L'Histoire du Costume Feminin Français de l'an 1037 a l'an 1870*, compiled by Paul Louis de Giafferri and published in 1929 by Editions Nilson, Paris. The book was printed by Georges Lang using letterpress for the text, and individually pulled impressions for the color illustrations, some involving up to twelve or thirteen passes, based on the number of different inks. The trim size measures some eleven by fifteen inches, and the number of illustrations is prodigious — it is difficult to conceive of such an illustrated book being produced today. Here, arranged chronologically from the Middle Ages through the Victorian era, are carefully catalogued and detailed examples of costumes and accessories including headdresses, millinery, gloves, shoes, and multilayered outfits from corsets to capes. Individual sections showing types of bodices, lace patterns, fabric designs, and embroidery details alternate with chapters cataloguing children's and infants' clothes. Umbrellas, handbags, and jewelry are included along with garments of every description.

It is evident from the slight variations in style that more than one artist was at work in producing this exhaustive volume, but it is difficult to find attributions by name. Illustrated leaves are signed with such names as "Misto," or "Vivette"; only the historical texts are uniformly signed with their authors' names. The interesting thing about this unusual source for Zelda's art is not so much its existence as historical material informing her own paper dolls, as the *changes* she wrought on this model. Zelda transformed these meticulously limned objects into figures that are far more fluid and lifelike, and imaginatively appealing than anything the devoted French artisans even approached. Inspired by this luxurious production's historical vividness, and its devotion to intricate observation, Zelda responded with her own devoted efforts to bring it to life.

Another book in Eleanor Lanahan's possession is a French volume from the 1920s, titled *L'Enfance de Becassine*, with text by "Camery," and illustrations by

J. Pinchon. Here again are illustrations with picturesque costumes, and a plethora of those modest appurtenances of everyday life that seem so appealing when they are removed by a little historical distance. Again, as is so evident in the de Giafferri historical illustrations, or even in the work of Boutet de Monvel or Arthur Rackham, to compare Zelda's figures with Pinchon's is to be reminded again of Zelda's superior draftsmanship and imaginative flair.

If the paper dolls and all their accompanying accoutrements constitute one of Zelda Fitzgerald's most satisfying achievements, it is in another aspect of her children's art that she synthesizes virtually every skill and talent honed in this work, and in the flower, figure, religious, and travel paintings. Six watercolor and gouache paintings (pp 86–93) probably made in 1941, depicting events from each of six chapters in *Alice's Adventures in Wonderland*, exemplify Zelda Fitzgerald's pictorial gifts at their highest pitch. Using every technique available to her — jarringly expressive color, dynamic composition and narrative complexity — the artist in these small pictures communicates on several levels. Lewis Carroll's story lines are concretely embedded in these paintings. Moreover, Carroll's double meanings, his trademark stamp of satire and his love of the absurd, come across loud and clear in these images. Zelda has not only deeply understood the subtext of *Alice in Wonderland*, but has visually translated, or better, found her own analogue to, the author's voice.

Despite their immense charm, and the clear ascendancy in Zelda Fitzgerald's oeuvre of the *Alice* pictures (together with others in this genre such as "The Three Little Pigs" or "The Three Little Kittens"), these works are far from being simply

accomplished illustrations, or delightful children's art. As a group, they convey undertones of darkness, and flashes of angry ambivalence. And they share a strange quality of almost willed imperfection. Compared to some of the flower paintings, and to the cityscapes of 1944, these pictures can seem at moments clumsy, idiosyncratic, with corners unresolved. If one imagines, however, these same compositions somehow "cleaned up," or purged of the flaws in color balance or proportion that haunt virtually every one of them, one begins to understand that without these peculiar awkwardnesses, they would lose some of their intensity. It is as though their author was consciously trying to transmit not only the story lines, but some of the tension, and the ambiguousness, inherent in the Lewis Carroll or Charles Perrault stories from which she was taking her departure.

The more one reads that most magnetic of children's books, *Alice's Adventures in Wonderland*, the more mysterious it becomes, the further its depths recede, and the more its improbable events enter into the domain of the inevitable. Something like this very same — internally contradictory — impulse fuels those best small, fiery paintings by Zelda Fitzgerald, whose glory arises from the timeless absurdity of *Alice*. Zelda cannot have missed the similarities between the adventures of the ever bemused heroine of Lewis Carroll's great adventure, and her own life.

Alice In Wonderland

In the forties, Zelda painted a series of fairy tales from Lewis Carroll's Alice's Adventures in Wonderland. The titles of the paintings are drawn from the chapters they illustrate.

Who Stole the Tarts?

Undated · Gouache on paper · 12 5/8 × 19 in.
Courtesy of Cecilia L. Ross

The King and Queen of Hearts were seated on their throne when they arrived, with a great crowd assembled about them — all sorts of little birds and beasts, as well as the whole pack of cards: the knave was standing before them, in chains, with a soldier on each side to guard him; and near the King was the White Rabbit, with a trumpet in one hand, and a scroll of parchment in the other. In the very middle of the court was a table, with a large dish of tarts upon it: they looked so good, that it made Alice quite hungry to look at them — 'I wish they'd get the trial done,' she thought, 'and hand round the refreshments!'

—*Alice's Adventures in Wonderland*

Overleaf · The Pool of Tears

Undated · Gouache on paper · 12 1/2 × 19 in.
Courtesy of Cecilia L. Ross

Alice cries so much and grows so small that she finds herself awash in a pool of tears.

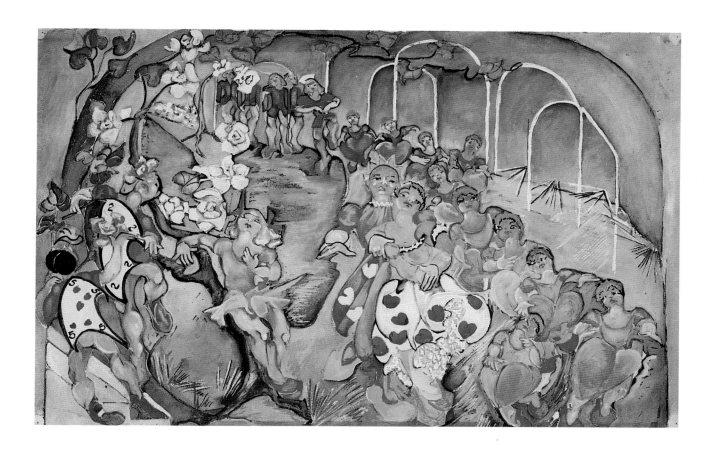

The Queen's Croquet-Ground

Undated · Gouache on paper · 12 1/4 × 19 3/8 in.
Courtesy of Eleanor Lanahan

Two began in a low voice, 'Why the fact is, you see, Miss, this here ought to have been a *red* rose-tree, and we put a white one in by mistake; and if the Queen was to find out, we should all have our heads cut off, you know. So you see, Miss, we're doing our best, afore she comes, to —'At this moment Five, who had been anxiously looking across the garden, called out 'The Queen! The Queen!'

—*Alice's Adventures in Wonderland*

Advice from a Caterpillar

Undated · Gouache on paper · 12 1/2 × 19 in.
Courtesy of Cecilia L. Ross

"Repeat, 'You are old, Father William,'" said the Caterpillar.
Alice folded her hands, and began:—
"'You are old, Father William,' the young man said,
'And your hair has become very white;
And yet you incessantly stand on your head —
Do you think, at your age, it is right?'
'In my youth,' Father William replied to his son,
'I feared it might injure the brain;
But, now that I'm perfectly sure I have none,
Why, I do it again and again....'"

—*Alice's Adventures in Wonderland*

A Mad Tea-Party

Undated · Gouache on paper · 12 1/2 × 19 in.
Courtesy of Eleanor Lanahan

There was a table set out under a tree in front of the house, and the March Hare and the Hatter were having tea at it: a dormouse was sitting between them, fast asleep…. The table was a large one, but the three were all crowded together at one corner of it: 'No room! No room!' they cried out when they saw Alice coming. 'There's plenty of room!' said Alice indignantly, and she sat down in a large arm-chair at one end of the table.

—*Alice's Adventures in Wonderland*

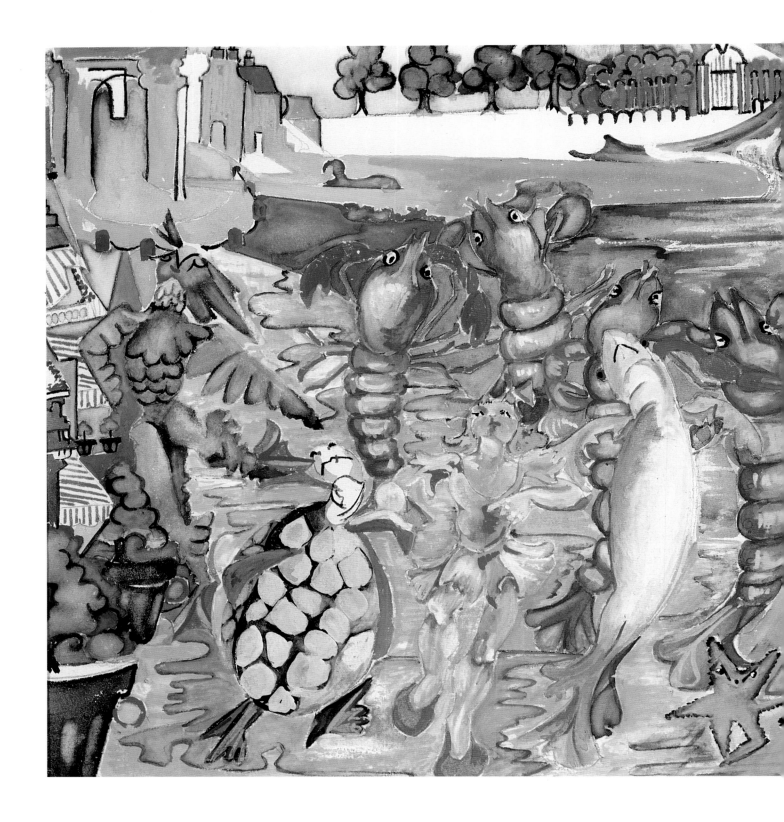

The Lobster Quadrille

Undated · Gouache on paper · 12 1/2 × 19 in.
Courtesy of Mrs Matthew J. Bruccoli

The Mock Turtle and the Gryphon demonstrate The Lobster Quadrille for Alice, a dance in which the lobsters are thrown out to sea. The Mock turtle sings of the snail's reluctance to join the dance:

"…What matters it how far we go?" his scaly friend replied.

"There is another shore, you know, upon the other side.

The further off from England the nearer is to France—

Then turn not pale, beloved snail, but come and join the dance…"

—*Alice's Adventures in Wonderland*

The background depicts Paris (left) and Nelson's Column in Trafalgar Square, London (right).

Fairy Tales

Although the fairy tales are undated, they were probably painted between 1943 and 1947.

The Three Little Pigs

Gouache on paper · 12 1/4 × 19 in.
Courtesy of Eleanor Lanahan

Goldilocks and the Three Bears

Gouache on paper · 12 1/4 × 19 in.
Courtesy of Cecilia L. Ross

Hansel and Gretel

Gouache on paper · 12 x 19 1/4 in.
Courtesy of Cecilia L. Ross

Puppeufée

Gouache on paper
11 1/2 × 18 3/4 in.
Courtesy of Eleanor Lanahan

Old Mother Hubbard

Gouache on paper · 12 × 19 in.
Courtesy of Cecilia L. Ross

Mary Had a Little Lamb

Gouache on paper · 11 1/2 x 18 3/4 in.
Courtesy of Eleanor Lanahan

Three Little Kittens Found Their Mittens

Gouache on paper · 12 1/4 × 19 1/2 in.
Courtesy of Eleanor Lanahan

The Little Man and the Little Maid

Gouache on paper · 12 1/2 x 19 3/4 in.
Courtesy of Cecilia L. Ross

Written on reverse:

> There was a little man
> And he loved a little maid
> And he said "little maid
> Will you wed—wed—wed?"
>
> But the little maid replied
> "Should I be your blushing bride
> Pray what should we have to eat—eat—eat?"
>
> "Will the flame that you're so rich in
> Light the fire in the kitchen
> Or the little God of love
> Turn the spit—spit—spit?"

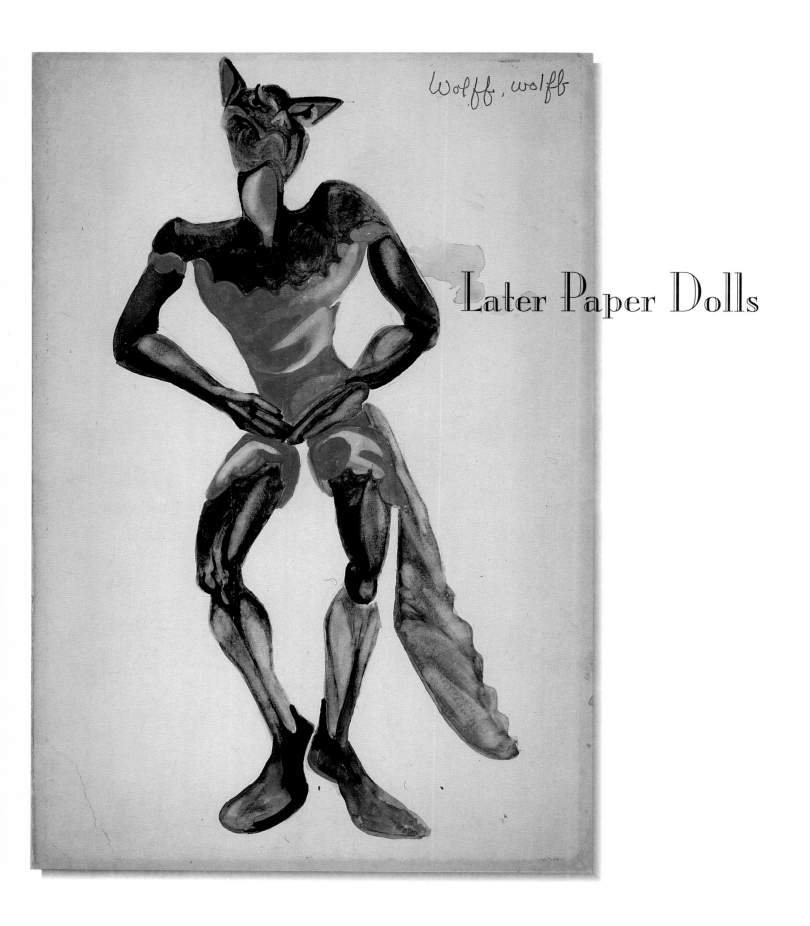

Wolff, wolff

Later Paper Dolls

Little Red Riding Hood

Gouache on poster board and paper
Courtesy of Cecilia L. Ross

(This series continues through page 108.)

"Wolff" costumes

Opposite · The "Wolff, Wolff"
14 1/2 in.

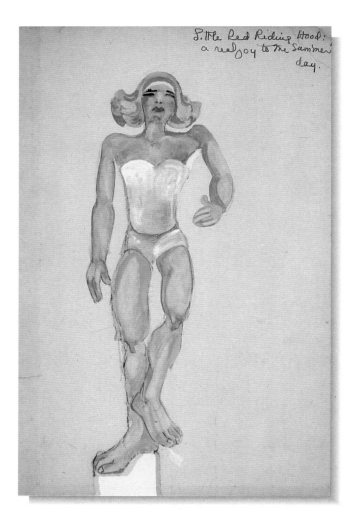

Little Red Riding Hood · 14 3/4 in.

Grandma · 14 1/4 in.

The Woodcutter · 15 in.

The Three Musketeers

Gouache on poster board and paper
Courtesy of Cecilia L. Ross

These figures represent characters from Alexandre Dumas's novel, *The Three Musketeers*, set in 1625 during the reign of Louis XIII.

Musketeer #1 · 14 3/4 in.

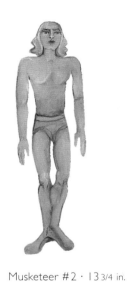

Musketeer #2 · 13 3/4 in.　　　　　　Musketeer #3 · 14 3/4 in.

Madame Bonacieux · 12 1/2 in.

Dumas recounts that as D'Artagnan leaves the masquerade ball, he is beckoned by a woman in a black velvet mask: "Despite this precaution, he recognized the alert, sprightly and shapely Madame Bonacieux."

Goldilocks and the Three Bears

Gouache on poster board and paper
Courtesy of Eleanor Lanahan

Goldilocks · 13 in.

Papa Bear · 13 in.

Mama Bear · 12 in.

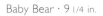

Baby Bear · 9 1/4 in.

Miscellaneous fairy-tale figures were among many unfinished characters discovered in Zelda's sketch pads.

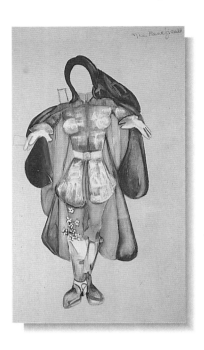

The Beneficent Queen · 13 7/8 in.
Courtesy of Eleanor Lanahan

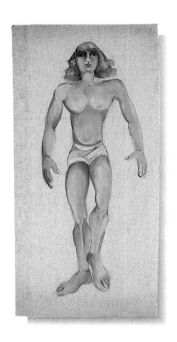

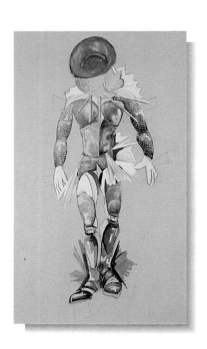

The Prince · 14 in.
Courtesy of Cecilia L. Ross

Witch · 14 1/4 in.

Witch's costume · 15 in.

Costume for The Good Fairy · 16 in.

Courtesy of Samuel J. Lanahan and Cecilia L. Ross

Zelda fashioned this two-sided pumpkin coach, hinged with wire brads, to serve as a portfolio for a series of paper dolls for her first grandchild, Thomas Lanahan, born in April 1946.

front

back

Pumpkin Coach

Gouache on heavy paper 14 1/2 x 16 1/2 in.
Courtesy of Cecilia L. Ross

In the mid-thirties Zelda experienced what she felt was a direct communication from God and remained deeply religious the rest of her life. From 1946 until 1948, Zelda worked on Bible illustrations for her first grandchild, Thomas Lanahan.

Adam and Eve

Late 1940s · Gouache on paper · 17 1/4 × 22 5/8 in.
Courtesy of Eleanor Lanahan

Star of Bethlehem

Late 1940s · Gouache on paper · 17 1/4 × 22 1/2 in.
Courtesy of Cecilia L. Ross

Written on reverse:

And thou Bethlehem, in the land of Juda,

Art not the least among the princes of Juda;

For out of thee shall come a governor,

that shall rule my people Israel

Marriage at Cana

Late 1940s · Gouache on paper · 17 1/4 × 22 5/8 in.
Courtesy of Cecilia L. Ross

Written on reverse:

> And the third day there was a marriage in Cana of Galilee; and the mother of Jesus was there;
> And both Jesus was called and his disciples to the marriage.
> And when they wanted wine, the mother of Jesus sayeth unto him
> they have no wine…
>
> Jesus saith unto them fill the waterpots with water.
> And they filled them up to the brim.
> And he saith unto them, draw out now and bear unto the governor of the feast. And they bear it.
>
> When the ruler of the feast had tasted the water that was
> made wine and knew not whence it was (but the servants knew)
> the governor of the feast called the bridegroom,
> And saith unto him… But thou hast kept the good wine until now.

The Parable of the Vineyard

Late 1940s · Gouache on paper · 17 x 22 in.
Courtesy of Cecilia L. Ross

Written on reverse:

...God command

There was a certain householder which planted a vineyard
...And let it out to husbandmen and went into a far country....
And when the time of the fruit drew near, he sent his servant
to the husbandmen, that they might receive the fruits of it

And the husbandmen took his servants, and beat one,
and killed another, and stoned another

...Last of all, he sent unto them his son, saying, they will reverence my son
But when the husbandmen saw the son, they ... cast him out of the vineyard and slew him.

The Deposition

c. 1945 · Watercolor and gouache on paper · 22 × 16 1/2 in.
Courtesy of the Montgomery Museum of Fine Arts

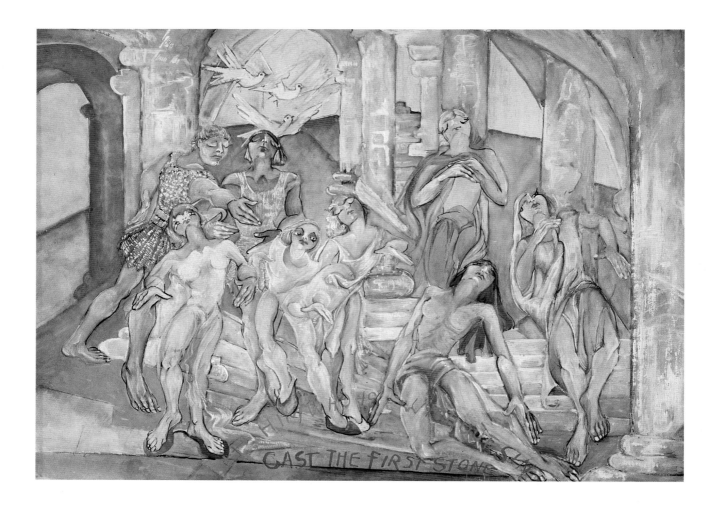

Let Him Who Is Without Sin Cast the First Stone

Late 1940s · Gouache on paper · 16 x 21 5/8 in.
Courtesy of Eleanor Lanahan

Written on reverse:

Do not commit adultery.

They said unto him master this woman was taken in adultery
Moses in the law commanded us, that such should be stoned

He said unto them let him who is without sin among you
first cast a stone

And Jesus was left alone, and the woman standing in the midst

Love One Another

Late 1940s · Gouache on paper
16 1/2 x 21 1/2 in.
Courtesy of Eleanor Lanahan

Written on reverse:

Now before the feast of the Passover, when Jesus knew that his hour was come That he should depart out of this world unto the Father having loved his own which were in the world, He loved them to the end.

Do Not Steal

Late 1940s · Gouache on paper
16 1/2 x 21 1/2 in.
Courtesy of Eleanor Lanahan

Written on reverse:

Lay not up treasures for yourselves on earth where moth and rust doth corrupt and thieves break through and steal

But lay up for yourselves treasures in heaven where neither moth nor rust doth corrupt and where thieves do not break through and steal

For where your treasure is
there will your heart be also

Chronology of Events in the Lives of Zelda and Scott Fitzgerald

September 24, 1896
Birth of F. Scott Fitzgerald in St Paul, Minnesota.

July 24, 1900
Birth of Zelda Sayre, a "child of the century," in Montgomery, Alabama.

1907
The Sayre family moves to 6 Pleasant Avenue, Zelda's home until 1920.

1909
Judge Sayre appointed Associate Justice of the Supreme Court of Ala.

September 1913
Scott enters Princeton University, class of 1917.

September 1916
Scott re-enters Princeton class of 1918 after a year's absence.

Spring 1917
Scott's poor academic record forces his withdrawal from Princeton before graduation.

October 1917
Scott receives his commission as 2nd lieutenant in the US Army.

March 1918
Scott completes draft of his first novel, The Romantic Egotist, *and submits it to Scribners. It is rejected.*

May 31, 1918
Zelda graduates from Sidney Lanier High School.

June 1918
Scott is billeted at Camp Sheridan near Montgomery, Ala.

July 1918
Zelda meets Scott at a country club dance.

February 1919
Scott is discharged from the Army and takes a job with an advertising company in New York City. He's engaged to marry Zelda.

June 1919
Zelda breaks her engagement to Scott.

September 1919
This Side of Paradise, an extensively revised version of The Romantic Egotist, *is accepted by Scribners.*

November 1919
Scott visits Zelda in Montgomery and they become engaged again.

March 26, 1920
Publication of This Side of Paradise.

April 3, 1920
Scott and Zelda are married in St Patrick's Cathedral, New York City. They honeymoon in Manhattan hotels.

May–September 1920
Scott and Zelda rent a house in Westport, Connecticut.

October 1920–April 1921
The Fitzgeralds live at 38 W. 59th Street, New York City.

May–July 1921
Scott and Zelda visit France, Italy, and England.

August 1921–September 1922
The Fitzgeralds settle in St Paul, Minnesota, for the birth of their daughter, Scottie, on October 26, 1921.

March 1922
Publication of Scott's second novel, The Beautiful and Damned.

April 2, 1922
Zelda's tongue-in-cheek review of The Beautiful and Damned, *"Friend Husband's Latest," appears in the* New York Tribune.

June 1922
Zelda's essay, "Eulogy on the Flapper," appears in Metropolitan Magazine.

September, 1922
Publication of Scott's collected short stories, Tales of the Jazz Age.

April 1924
The Fitzgerald family sets sail for France.

June 1924
The family rents Villa Marie, in St Raphaël. Zelda has an involvement with a French aviator, Edouard Jozan. Scott works on The Great Gatsby.

Winter 1924–1925
The Fitzgeralds move to Rome where Scott revises The Great Gatsby.

October 1924
Zelda's short essay, "Does A Moment of Revolt Come Sometime to Every Married Man?" appears in McCall's.

February 1925
The Fitzgeralds vacation in Capri, where Zelda may have taken her first painting lessons.

April 1925
Publication of The Great Gatsby.

June 1925
"Our Own Movie Queen," appears in the Chicago Sunday Tribune, *attributed to Scott but, he noted in his ledger, two-thirds by Zelda.*

May–December 1925
The family rents an apartment in Paris.

October 1925
"What Became of the Flappers?" by Zelda, appears in McCall's *opposite Scott's, "Our Young Rich Boys."*

August 1925
The Fitzgeralds vacation in Antibes.

March–December 1926
The Fitzgeralds rent a villa in Juan-les-Pins on the Riviera.

December 1926
The family returns to America.

January 1927
Scott and Zelda stay in Hollywood where Scott works on the screenplay for Lipstick.

March 1927–March 1928
The Fitzgeralds rent Ellerslie near Wilmington, Delaware. Zelda takes art and dance lessons in Philadelphia.

April 1928
The family returns to Paris for the summer. Zelda studies ballet with Lubov Egorova, director of dance for the Diaghilev Ballet.

September 1928–March 1929
The Fitzgeralds again rent Ellerslie in Delaware.

Winter 1928–1929
Zelda writes five stories for College Humor, *including, "Looking Back Eight Years," and Scott's name appears as co-author to get quadruple the fee.*

March 1929
The family returns to France.

May 1929
Under Scott's name, Zelda's article, "Paint and Powder," appears in The Smart Set.

June 1929
The family travels to Cannes where Zelda continues with ballet. She declines an invitation to dance Aida with the Royal Ballet of Italy.

July 1929
"Southern Girl," and "The Original Follies Girl," appear in College Humor with Scott's byline although written by Zelda.

October 1929
The Fitzgeralds return to their apartment in Paris. Zelda resumes her study of ballet with Lubov Egorova.

February 1930
Scott and Zelda take a holiday in North Africa. Her story, "The Girl the Prince Liked," appears in College Humor.

April 1930
Zelda is hospitalized for "nervous exhaustion" at Malmaison Clinic near Paris. Her story, "The Girl with Talent," appears in College Humor.

May 1930
"A Millionaire's Girl," with Scott's byline but written by Zelda, appears in the Saturday Evening Post.

June 1930
Zelda enters Prangins Clinic near Geneva, Switzerland, where she is diagnosed as schizophrenic. She gives up ballet.

January 1931
"Poor Working Girl," with Scott's byline but written by Zelda, appears in College Humor.

September 1931
Zelda is discharged from Prangins. The family returns to Montgomery, Ala.

September 1931–Spring 1932
They rent 819 Felder Ave. in Montgomery. Scott spends three months in Hollywood alone, working on Red-Headed Woman.

December 1931
Zelda's story, "Miss Ella," appears in Scribner's Magazine.

February 1932
Zelda suffers her second breakdown and enters Phipps Psychiatric Clinic, part of Johns Hopkins Hospital in Baltimore.

May 1932–November 1933
Scott rents La Paix near Baltimore.

June 1932
Zelda is discharged from Phipps and joins family at La Paix.

August 1932
Zelda's story, "A Couple of Nuts," appears in Scribner's Magazine.

October 1932
Publication of Zelda's novel, Save Me The Waltz.

June 1933
Production of Zelda's play, Scandalabra, by Vagabond Junior Players in Baltimore.

October 1933
Zelda enters the Independent Artists' Exhibition at the Baltimore Museum of Art.

November–December 1933
Scott and Zelda vacation in Bermuda.

January 1934
Zelda suffers her third breakdown and enters Sheppard-Pratt Hospital near Baltimore.

March 1934
Zelda transfers to Craig House in Beacon, New York.

March 29–April 30, 1934
Zelda's exhibition at the Cary Ross Gallery in Manhattan.

April 1934
Publication of Scott's fourth novel, Tender Is The Night.

May 1934
Zelda transfers to Sheppard-Pratt Hospital.

May–July 1934
Zelda's articles, "Auction — Model 1934" and "Show Mr. and Mrs. F. to Number___" appear in Esquire.

May 1935
Scott spends the summer at Grove Park Inn, Asheville, N.C.

September 1935
Scott rents an apartment with Scottie at Cambridge Arms, Baltimore.

April 1936
Zelda enters Highland Hospital in Asheville, North Carolina.

July–December 1936
Scott lives at Grove Park Inn to be near Zelda.

January–June 1937
Scott lives at Oak Hall Hotel in Tryon.

July 1937
Scott returns to Hollywood for the last time. He works for MGM as a screenwriter.

September 1937
Scott and Zelda visit Myrtle Beach and Charleston, S.C.

March 1938
The Fitzgerald family spends a week at the Cavalier Hotel in Virginia Beach, VA.

September 1938
Scottie enters Vassar.

December 1938
Scott's contract with MGM is not renewed.

February 1939
Zelda takes month-long courses in costume design and life drawing at the Ringling School of Art in Sarasota, Florida. Later this year she exhibits with the Asheville Artists' Guild.

April 1940
Zelda leaves Highland Hospital to live with her mother at 322 Sayre Street in Montgomery. She returns to Highland, intermittently, for the rest of her life.

December 21 1940
Scott dies of a heart attack at Sheilah Graham's apartment, 1443 Hayworth Avenue, Hollywood.

December 27 1940
Scott is buried at the Rockville Union Cemetery, Rockville, Maryland. Zelda is not able to attend.

October 1941
Posthumous publication of The Last Tycoon.

May 1942
Zelda's art is exhibited at the Montgomery Museum of Fine Arts.

December 1942
Zelda's art is exhibited at the Woman's Club in Montgomery.

March 10 1948
Zelda dies in a fire at Highland Hospital, Asheville, N.C. She is buried with Scott in the Rockville Union Cemetery, Rockville, Maryland.

Notes

Central Park

The following abbreviations are used:
ZSF — Zelda Sayre Fitzgerald
FSF — Francis Scott Fitzgerald
SFS or Scottie — Frances Fitzgerald Lanahan Smith

Notes for the Introduction

Page

11   "Both of us are very splashy": ZSF to FSF, February 1920, *Correspondence of F. Scott Fitzgerald*, ed. Matthew J. Bruccoli, and Margaret M. Duggan (New York: Random House, 1980), p. 52.

11   "One could get away with more": FSF, *The Crack-Up*, ed. Edmund Wilson (New York: New Directions, 1945), p. 19.

12   "Yellow roses she bought with her money": ZSF, *Save Me the Waltz* (New York: Charles Scribner's Sons, 1932), p. 185.

12   "Twilights were wonderful just after the war": ZSF, "A Millionaire's Girl" first appeared in the *Saturday Evening Post* May 7, 1930. Bylined FSF, but credited to ZSF in his ledger. *Zelda Fitzgerald: The Collected Writings*, ed. Matthew J. Bruccoli (New York: Charles Scribner's Sons, 1991), p. 327.

13   "In those days of going to pieces": ZSF, "A Couple of Nuts" first published in *Scribner's Magazine*, August 1932. *Zelda Fitzgerald: The Collected Writings*, Bruccoli, p. 460.

13   "Every day it seems to me that things are more barren": ZSF to FSF, 1930/31, Nancy Milford, *Zelda: A Biography* (New York: Harper & Row, 1970), p. 166.

13   "If all the kisses and love I'm sending": ZSF to FSF, 1930/31, *Zelda Fitzgerald: The Collected Writings*, Bruccoli, p. 460.

13   "The moon slips into the mountains like a lost": ZSF to FSF, Fall 1930, *Zelda Fitzgerald: The Collected Writings*, Bruccoli, p. 458.

13   "When I came down the hill the moon was still": ZSF to FSF, 1930, *Correspondence of F. Scott Fitzgerald*, Bruccoli and Duggan, p. 252.

14   "I have often told you that I am that little fish": ZSF to FSF, March 1932, *Zelda Fitzgerald: The Collected Writings*, Bruccoli, p. 465.

14   "Please ask Mrs. Owens": ZSF to FSF, March 1934, *Correspondence of F. Scott Fitzgerald.*, Bruccoli and Duggan, p. 335.

15   "Dear: I am not trying to make": ZSF to FSF, 1934, *Zelda Fitzgerald: The Collected Writings*, Bruccoli, p. 470.

15   "We saw Georgia O'Keeffe's pictures": ZSF "Show Mr. and Mrs. F. to Number __" Published in *Esquire*. Bylined by FSF but credited to ZSF in his ledger, May–June 1934. *Zelda Fitzgerald: The Collected Writings*, Bruccoli, p. 431.

15   "I had few friends but I <u>never</u> quarreled": ZSF to Scottie, Milford, *Zelda*, p. 373.

15   "Yes — but David, it's very difficult": ZSF, *Save Me the Waltz*, p. 73.

16   "The Sheppard-Pratt Hospital is located": ZSF to FSF, October 1934. *Correspondence of F. Scott Fitzgerald*, Bruccoli and Duggan, p. 388.

16   "You are the finest, loveliest, tenderest": FSF to ZSF, May 6, 1939, *A Life in Letters*, ed. Matthew J. Bruccoli (New York: Charles Scribner's Sons, 1994) p. 391.

16   "I don't write; and I don't paint": ZSF to FSF, 1940, Milford, *Zelda*, p. 343.

17   "There isn't any real reason": ZSF to Scottie, Milford, *Zelda*, pp. 373–374.

Above · Wooden Bowls

c. 1944–1945 · Oil on wood · 6 1/4 in. diameter
Courtesy of Eleanor Lanahan

To earn "pin money," Zelda painted dozens of wooden bowls.

Brooklyn Bridge

Place de l'Opera

Notes for "A Portrait of Zelda Fitzgerald"

Page

19   "I don't need anything except hope": ZSF, Scott Donaldson, *Fool for Love* (New York: Congdon & Weed, Inc., 1983), p. 95.

19   "I've spent to-day in the grave-yard": ZSF to FSF, Spring 1919, Andrew Turnbull, *Scott Fitzgerald* (New York: Charles Scribner's Sons, 1962), p. 94.

19   "It was despair, despair, despair": quoted in Malcolm Cowley's Introduction to *The Bodley Head Scott Fitzgerald* (London: The Bodley Head Ltd., 1963), p. 29.

19   "In a real dark night of the soul it is always three o'clock in the morning": FSF, "Handle With Care," *The Crack-Up*, ed. Edmund Wilson (New York: New Directions, 1945,) p. 75.

19   "He couldn't have found a book of his": SFS, Introduction to *Letters To his Daughter*, ed. Andrew Turnbull, (New York: Charles Scribner's Sons, 1965), p. xi.

19   "The world angered God with vanities": ZSF undated, unpublished letter, copies of which she sent to numerous friends including Mrs. Eben Finney.

20   "There goes that crazy woman": Nancy Milford, "The Golden Dreams of Zelda Fitzgerald," *Harper's Magazine*, January 1969, p. 46.

20   "Didn't see people anymore": Milford, "The Golden Dreams of Zelda Fitzgerald," *Harper's Magazine*, January 1969, p. 46.

20   "Of course at first she was invited": Milford, "The Golden Dreams of Zelda Fitzgerald," *Harper's Magazine*, January 1969, p. 52.

20   "I reconciled myself and had to accept": ZSF to Anne Ober, June 26, 1945, Nancy Milford, *Zelda: A Biography* (New York: Harper & Row, 1970), p. 373.

20   "When Zelda Sayre came to dances": Edward Pattillo, Introduction to catalogue of ZSF exhibition at the Montgomery Museum of Fine Arts, Sept. 1974, p. 10.

20   "She has the straightest nose": *Montgomery Advertiser*, Milford, *Zelda*, p. 15.

20   "I did not have a single feeling of inferiority": ZSF's Prangins records, 1930/31, Milford, *Zelda*, p. 8.

20   "She lived on the cream at the top": Milford, *Zelda*, p. 16.

21   "The Ohio troops have started a wild": ZSF to FSF, Milford, *Zelda*, p. 44.

21   "And I want to be married soon": ZSF to FSF, *Correspondence of F. Scott Fitzgerald*, ed. Matthew J. Bruccoli, and Margaret M. Duggan (New York: Random House, 1980,) p. 44.

21   "I've always known that any girl who gets stewed": Milford, *Zelda*, p. 60.

21   "Eleanor Browder and I have found": ZSF to FSF, circa 1919, Princeton University Library.

21   "Scott, you're really awful silly": ZSF to FSF, Milford, *Zelda*, p. 45.

21   "Zelda was cagey about throwing in her lot": Donaldson, *Fool for Love*, p. 64.

21   "It will take more than the pope": Minnie Sayre, Sara Mayfield, *The Constant Circle* (New York: Delacorte Press, 1968), p. 37.

21   "Don't you think I was made for you?": ZSF to FSF, circa 1919, Princeton University Library.

21   "I'm absolutely nothing without you": ZSF to FSF, Feb. 1920, *Correspondence of F. Scott Fitzgerald*, Bruccoli and Duggan, p. 51.

22   "The most charming person in the world": *Louisville Courier-Journal*, "What a 'Flapper Novelist' Thinks of His Wife," Sept. 30, 1923.

22   "I am assuming that the Flapper": ZSF, "Euology on the Flapper," 1922, *Zelda Fitzgerald: The Collected Writings*, ed. Matthew Bruccoli (New York: Macmillan,1991,) p. 391.

22   "Did you ever see a woman's face": ZSF, Turnbull, *Scott Fitzgerald*, p. 165–166.

22   "Capacity for carrying things off": Edmund Wilson, Bruccoli, *Some Sort of Epic Grandeur*, p. 136.

22   "The arch type of what New York wanted": FSF, *The Crack-Up*, p. 26.

22   "When Zelda Sayre and I were young": Donaldson, *Fool For Love*, p. 66.

22   "It was an age of miracles": FSF, *The Crack-Up*, p. 14.

22   "I was in love with a whirlwind": FSF, Milford, *Zelda*, p. 52.

22   "I hate a room without an open": Donaldson, *Fool for Love*, p. 96.

22   "I like men to be just incidents": ZSF to FSF, April 1919, Milford, *Zelda*, p. 48.

22   "If I had anything to do with creating": FSF, Cowley, *The Bodley Head Scott Fitzgerald*, p. 16.

22   "Youth does not need friends": ZSF, "Euology on the Flapper," 1922, *Zelda Fitzgerald: The Collected Writings*, Bruccoli, p. 391.

22   "Sometimes I don't know whether Zelda": FSF, Cowley, *The Bodley Head Scott Fitzgerald*, p. 16.

22   "All I want is to be very young always": ZSF, Milford, *Zelda*, p. 59.

22   "Recognized a portion of an old diary": ZSF, "Mrs. F. Scott Fitzgerald Reviews 'The Beautiful and Damned,'" *New York Tribune*, Apr. 2, 1922.

22   "He endowed those years that might have": ZSF to Mrs. Eben Finney, (collection of Peaches McPherson), undated.

23   "I never thought she was beautiful": Dorothy Parker, Milford, *Zelda*, p. 68.

23   "And the first thing that struck me": Kenneth Tynan, "Profile of Louise Brooks, *New Yorker*, June 11, 1979, p. 71.

23   "She talked with so spontaneous color": Edmund Wilson, *The Portable Edmund Wilson*, ed. Lewis M. Dabney (New York: Viking Press, 1983), p. 191.

23   "The best flapper is reticent emotionally": ZSF, "What Became of the Flappers?", 1925, *Zelda Fitzgerald: The Collected Writings*, Bruccoli, p. 398.

23   "A world of nannies and beach umbrellas": ZSF, Turnbull, *Scott Fitzgerald*, p. 157.

23   "We don't go in for self-preservation": ZSF & FSF, Turnbull, *Scott Fitzgerald*, p. 181.

24   "Very alcoholic & chaotic time": ZSF, Turnbull, *Scott Fitzgerald*, p. 132.

24   "The strangeness and excitement of New York": ZSF to FSF 1930, *Zelda Fitzgerald: The Collected Writings*, Bruccoli, p. 451.

24   "Darling heart, — I won't drink *any* if you object": ZSF to FSF, Milford, *Zelda*, p. 47.

24   "You can drink some of the cocktails": Turnbull, *Scott Fitzgerald*, p. 165.

24   "Because the world is chaos and when I drink": ZSF, Turnbull, *Scott Fitzgerald*, p. 193.

24   "Just seen the doom of youth": Turnbull, *Scott Fitzgerald*, p. 136.

24   "I have cat thoughts that chase the mice": ZSF to Dr Mildred Squires, 1932, Milford, *Zelda*, pp. 212–213.

25   "One day in 1926 we looked down and found": FSF, *The Crack-Up*, p. 26.

25   "Not that one was frightened from one's own": Milford, *Zelda*, p. 99.

25   "Now Ludlow, take it from an old souse": ZSF to Ludlow Fowler, Turnbull, *Scott Fitzgerald*, p. 168.

25   "Full of the sun ... the head of the gold of a Christmas coin": ZSF, *Save me the Waltz*, reprinted in *Zelda Fitzgerald: The Collected Writings*, Bruccoli, p. 80.

25   "That if he were away she could sleep with another man": ZSF to FSF, Donaldson, *Fool For Love*, p. 68.

25   "Zelda and I close together. Trouble clearing": FSF's *Ledger*, Turnbull, *Scott Fitzgerald*, p. 146.

25   "There were four or five Zeldas": James Thurber, *Credos and Curios* (New York: Harper & Row, 1962), p. 154.

25   "To stay married and in love with": Turnbull, *Scott Fitzgerald*, p. 172.

26   "Something of her own": ZSF, *Save Me the Waltz*, reprinted in *Zelda Fitzgerald: The Collected Writings*, Bruccoli, p. 118.

26   "I think you'll see that apart from the beauty and richness of the writing": FSF to Maxwell Perkins, May 1, 1930, *Dear Scott/Dear Max*, ed. John Kuehl and Jackson Bryer (New York: Charles Scribner's Sons, 1971), p. 167.

26   "She no longer read or thought": FSF to Dr. Oscar Forel, 1930, Bruccoli, *Some Sort of Epic Grandeur*, p. 197.

26   "I began to like Egorova": ZSF to FSF late summer/early fall 1930, *Zelda Fitzgerald: The Collected Writings*, Bruccoli, p. 454.

26   "Bogus ... a pansy with hair on his chest": Sara Mayfield, *Exiles from Paradise* (New York: Delacorte Press, 1971) pp. 137, 141.

26   "It's frightful, it's horrible, what's going to become of me": ZSF, Bruccoli, *Some Sort of Epic Grandeur*, p. 342.

26   "A constitutional, emotionally unbalanced psychopath": Milford, *Zelda*, p.179.

26   "A great imbecile": Milford, *Zelda*, p. 179.

27   "I seem awfully queer to myself": ZSF to FSF, Milford, *Zelda*, p. 177.

27   "I can't help clinging to the idea": FSF to Dr Oscar Forel, 1931, *F. Scott Fitzgerald: A Life in Letters*, ed. Matthew Bruccoli (New York: Scribners, 1994), p. 206.

27   "Try to understand that people are not always reasonable": ZSF to FSF from Prangins, Milford, *Zelda*, p. 185.

27   "Could have chewed sticks": ZSF, Turnbull, *Scott Fitzgerald*, p. 195.

27   "I cannot consider one pint of wine": FSF to Dr Forel,1930, *F. Scott Fitzgerald: A Life in Letters*, Bruccoli, p. 197.

27   "Probably be carried off eventually": FSF to Dr Adolph Meyer,1932, *F. Scott Fitzgerald: A Life in Letters*, Bruccoli, p. 228.

28   "Now that I can't sleep anymore": ZSF to FSF late summer/early fall,1930, *Zelda Fitzgerald: The Collected Writings*, Bruccoli, p. 456.

28   "Nothing but the troubles that were reflected in our relations": SFS, Introduction to *Letters To His Daughter*, ed. Andrew Turnbull (New York: Charles Scribner's Sons, 1965), p. xi.

28   "What I might have been and done is lost, spent, gone, dissipated": FSF, *The Crack-Up*, p. 67.

28   "It's a script that reads well": SFS, Introduction to catalogue for ZSF exhibition at Montgomery Museum of Fine Arts, Sept. 1974, p. 4.

28   "Turning up in a novel signed by my wife": FSF to Dr Mildred Squires, March 14, 1932, *F. Scott Fitzgerald: A Life in Letters*, Bruccoli, p. 209.

29   "You are a third-rate writer and a third-rate ballet dancer": FSF to ZSF, Bruccoli, *Some Sort of Epic Grandeur*, p. 409.

29   "It seems to me that you are making a rather violent attack": Bruccoli, *Some Sort of Epic Grandeur*, p. 410.

29   "A great artist or a great anything": ZSF to FSF, 1934, *Zelda Fitzgerald: The Collected Writings*, Bruccoli, p. 470.

29   "The will-to-power": ZSF to FSF, 1934, *Zelda Fitzgerald: The Collected Writings*, Bruccoli, p. 470.

29   "It was my mother's misfortune": SFS, Introduction to catalogue for ZSF exhibit at Montgomery Museum of Fine Arts, Sept. 1974, p. 5.

29   "You talk of the function of art": *Zelda Fitzgerald: The Collected Writings*, Bruccoli, p. 475.

29   "Worry about critics — what sorrows have they": ZSF to FSF, April 1934, *Zelda Fitzgerald: The Collected Writings*, Bruccoli, p. 472.

29   "Inexhaustible store of efforts": ZSF to FSF, Fall 1939, *Correspondence of F. Scott Fitzgerald*, Bruccoli and Duggan, p. 556.

29   "You are all I care about on earth": ZSF to FSF, Nov. 1931, *Correspondence of F. Scott Fitzgerald*, Bruccoli and Duggan, p. 271.

29   "I can carry most of contemporary literary opinion": FSF to ZSF, April 26, 1934, *Correspondence of F. Scott Fitzgerald*, Bruccoli and Duggan, p. 356.

29   "The insane are merely guests on earth": FSF, May 7, 1940, *Letters to His Daughter*, p. 163.

29   "I have asked a lot of my emotions —": FSF, *The Crack-Up*, p. 165.

Endnotes for "On the Art of Zelda Fitzgerald"

1.   Matthew J. Bruccoli, ed., *Zelda Fitzgerald: The Collected Writings* (New York: Macmillan Publishing Company, 1991), p. 401.

2.   Bruccoli, p. 349.

3.   Nancy Milford, *Zelda: A Biography* (New York: Harper & Row, Inc., 1970), p. 141.

4.   A document found in the accession files of the Montgomery Museum of Fine Arts details the circumstance of a body of work expressly destroyed by the artist. E. Herndon, History Consultant to the Mobile Public Library wrote in a letter to the museum dated March 13, 1973: "During 1942 I had organized several groups of artists who were stationed at various (army) fields in Alabama.... I obtained a place for them to work, but they did not have funds to buy materials for their work. I mentioned this to Zelda. Her response was immediate. She asked me to go with her to her mother's house. When we arrived there we went to the garage.... The Garage was full of her paintings. She told me ... that she wanted me to give these paintings to the artists in the group. However, she stated that the pictures were never to be shown as her work, and that anyone receiving them was to paint over them, or remove the pictures with paint remover and use the canvas for their own work. The canvases were of the finest linen and the pictures were painted in France. There were about twenty pictures in that garage...." Courtesy Carolyn Shafer, "To Spread a Human Aspiration: The Art of Zelda Sayre Fitzgerald," Master of Arts Thesis in the Department of Art, University of South Carolina, 1994.]

5.   One demonstrated sign of the reluctance of the art establishment to acknowledge, or even to look at, her work as more than an eccentric and dismissable episode in American art of the twentieth century, has been the recent difficulty of persuading mainstream art museums to present an exhibition of Zelda Fitzgerald's work. When, at last, both the holdings of the Montgomery Museum and the family, have been discriminatingly brought together and offered for exhibition, the reaction of most of the seemingly appropriate institutions, has been bafflingly indifferent. Perhaps this is a comparable resistance to that of the establishment's initial indifference to the literary achievement.

6.   Milford, p. 335.

7.   Carolyn Shafer quoting Jerry and Robbie Tillotson, "Zelda Fitzgerald Still Lives," *The Feminist Art Journal*, vol. 4 (Spring 1975), p. 32.

8.   Carolyn Shafer, "To Spread a Human Aspiration: The Art of Zelda Sayre Fitzgerald," unpublished Master of Arts dissertation, Department of Art, Universtiy of South Carolina, 1994, p. 102.

9.   Milford, p. 137.

10.   From a letter to Maxwell Perkins, March 1941, Charles Scribner's Sons Papers, Dept. of Rare Books and Special Collections, Princeton University Libraries. It seems likely that Zelda thought on more than this occasion of publishing this kind of work.